A SEASON TO SAVOUR

Edward Skingsley

ISBN 9781523895021

DEDICATION

This book is dedicated to my Mum.

In her 86th year, and sadly not in the best of health, she was the friendly but dark force that always wanted to seek, remove and destroy the contents of an old suitcase in my bedroom - namely my old North End bits and pieces collection. I argued it was history. She said they were just old bits of paper. No way did I leave the key lying around.

Her mission even lasted into my adulthood but diminished instantly when I chanced upon her outrageously large assortment of knitting patterns when helping her move house.

Rumbled, she then laughingly revealed how she had actually worked on the 'North End Desk' at Mather Bros in the 50's, (then North End's official programme printer), and indeed liaised with club when they telephoned the team through, adding *"It was always handy when you needed tickets for a big game..."*

Stunned, open mouthed and rendered speechless at this spontaneous confession, she instantly regaled me with past North End tales of legend and wonder; a trip to the 1954 FA Cup Semi Final at Maine Road, sourcing tickets for the Final through the club, the Derek Dooley game, Tom Finney's exploits, swearing the printers to secrecy when they knew Finney's name wasn't going on the team sheet that weekend, she even recited the 50's team parrot fashion!

There was more, much more.

"So, after all that, why did you always want to throw my North End stuff out?!?!"

The reply by the Football Memorabilia Assassin was brief, ruthless and delivered with tempo.

"Because I wanted THAT suitcase for THESE knitting patterns."

A SEASON TO SAVOUR

ACKNOWLEDGMENTS

Preston North End Football Club and the Lancashire Evening Post for their kind permission to use information and photographs from their past publications. Special thanks to Ben Rhodes and Mike Hill.

Special thanks to Graham Hawkins for contributing the Foreword

Thanks to Kevin Williamson for displaying his proof reading skills

Thanks to Ian Rigby and Mike Payne for their encouragement

Thanks to Toffs for allowing me to use the image of their Preston North End 1970 shirt badge

A SEASON TO SAVOUR

CONTENTS

A SEASON TO SAVOUR

FOREWORD

That special season of 1970/71 certainly brings back fantastic memories for me.

Looking back, Alan Ball welcomed us that season by not even showing us a football for a couple of weeks, it was run, run and run some more. He shouted at us from the sidelines that it would benefit us and we would be stronger. Although we didn't appreciate it at the time, he was right as our end of season stamina carried us through.

Arthur Cox was Bally's right hand man, and their preparation for games was meticulous. We knew what the opposition would try to do but more importantly we knew what we had to do. We also had to know and understand our teammates jobs too - not just our own. Those Friday morning pre-match meetings were so long they would sometimes see Bally get through a full packet of 20 cigarettes!

I seem to recall that Alan Spavin wasn't included in the first few line ups, but it didn't take long for Bally to realise that he could really play, take on responsibility and be a leader in the dressing room. As the season progressed he really came into his own and was eventually named as the division's outstanding player. Alan Kelly was another player who was strong in the dressing room and on the pitch, and of course there was George Ross, who was quite simply North End to the bone. Alongside me was John Bird - what a great signing! Strong minded and wanted to learn. A good team needs such characters.

The game at Fulham was an unbelievable experience. It was extremely hard work but a wonderful outcome and really laid the championship on a platter for us. We were prepared very well by Bally for that final game against Rotherham United and there was no way we were not lifting that title!

I was very proud to be North End captain at that special time, and that pride stays with me even today.

Having read a sneak preview of the book, I am sure you are going to enjoy it. It paints a very good picture from a supporter's point of view, bringing in all the tension and excitement of that great season.

Graham Hawkins, captain of Preston North End 1970/71

Setting the Scene

Decline, 1969/70, Alan Ball Senior Arrives, Pre-Season Fixtures, Transfer Rumours, Ready to Go

It took precisely a decade, neatly packaged as *'The 60's'* for Preston North End to wither away from enjoying a relatively healthy Division One status in 1959/60, to becoming relegation fodder in Division Two during 1969/70. Admittedly, there was a good diversion or two along the way – 1963/64 for instance. That season, they finished 3rd in Division Two and reached the FA Cup Final - no mean feat - only to lose in the last few minutes 3-2 to West Ham United. However, this and a few good cup runs apart, a line graph of North End's performance in the 60's would demonstrate a club latterly suffering a severe bout of apathy and in modern parlance, 'heading south' - rapidly.

That decade closing season, 1969/70, was an unmitigated disaster. I vividly recall watching at Deepdale that season and it was quite obvious that there was no heart or real fight at all from the team as they hovered all season in and around the drop zone. Lurching from defeat to defeat in the 'run-in', fate decided it would be our old adversaries,

Blackpool, who would put the 'tin hat' on our campaign.

A display that was the polar opposite of North End's saw them win 3-0 at Deepdale – the memory of looking directly at an ecstatic Fred Pickering hanging in the North End net from my Kop vantage point making it extremely difficult to keep my tea down! The North End fans largely walked away in silence that night, as the Blackpool fans were taunting that, 'This is the end of PNE...' A dreadful experience!

It was completely unacceptable. After all, a net seven points taken from the last 32 available, smacks of giving up, lying down and rolling over. Behind the scenes, things were apparently even more chaotic. The plain, unvarnished truth was that Preston North End were something of a shambles.

This was the era when the bigger city and conurbation clubs were finding the right type of lasting investment to move onwards and upwards leaving the smaller town clubs behind. North End's plight wasn't going to be unique; indeed in the following few seasons all their close neighbours would suffer a similar indignity.

As always, in those dark days of unspectacular financial planning, the mole gnawing at the backside of these smaller, 'high risk' clubs was the bank. They would insist at random times that they wanted to call in some debt, so the club in question had no option but to move on their best players. Performances declined, fans became frustrated and crowds fell away. Unearth a new star and the vicious circle started again. Clubs that eventually started the journey into decline would find their role defined at best to be a 'feeder' for the big clubs.

As soon as the final whistle blew on that fateful evening of April 13th 1970, the incumbent Manager, Bobby Seith and the coach, Bryan Edwards had their warrants signed after a hastily arranged meeting of the North End board. They were rubber stamped and duly delivered at the scheduled board meeting on the Thursday evening, with North End immediately advertising in the press for replacements.

For the remaining match, a couple of nominated senior players would assist Chairman Tom Nicholson with team selection while ex-full back Willie Cunningham put his hand up, volunteering to be temporary Trainer.

Within a few days, two players felt unsettled enough to consider their futures at Deepdale, both handing in transfer requests.

Reserve goalkeeper, Gerry Stewart put in his transfer request to the board shortly after Bobby Seith was sacked, citing a desire for first team football as the reason. Stewart was highly rated at Deepdale; indeed Seith had recommended him for a Scotland U23 Cap during the season.

The other player to have asked for a move was Graham Hawkins. Far from accepting the request, the board asked the player to reconsider carefully his options as they would almost certainly want to retain his services. One or two other players were reported to be considering matters too...

Tom Finney even had his say. In a *Lancashire Evening Post* (LEP) interview, he said he was frightened that North End's gradual decline would lead to years in the Third Division wilderness – citing Luton Town's eight year struggle to scramble out of it. He added, *"Serious mistakes have been made at both management and board level, and quite frankly I don't think the board have been 'with it.' They have lived in the past for too long, bemoaning the situation that faced them without really doing anything about it."*

Those words just about summed it all up.

With the fans in limbo for a few weeks, speculation was mounting about just who would take over the management reins – and history shows that on this occasion the board of directors made the correct decision. They appointed Alan Ball Senior, manager of Halifax Town, father of the England international and World Cup winner and a coach desperate to move onwards and upwards and hungry for success. He had moved the West Yorkshire club to relative safety in Division Three from the depths of Division Four in just a couple of years.

The LEP reported that, *"North End can consider themselves somewhat fortunate to receive 60 applications for the vacant post. The board of directors considered Ball by far the best of the bunch. Certainly North End could not get a more dedicated professional. Ball lives for football, his knowledge of the game is second to none and he could well be the man to lift the Deepdale depression."*

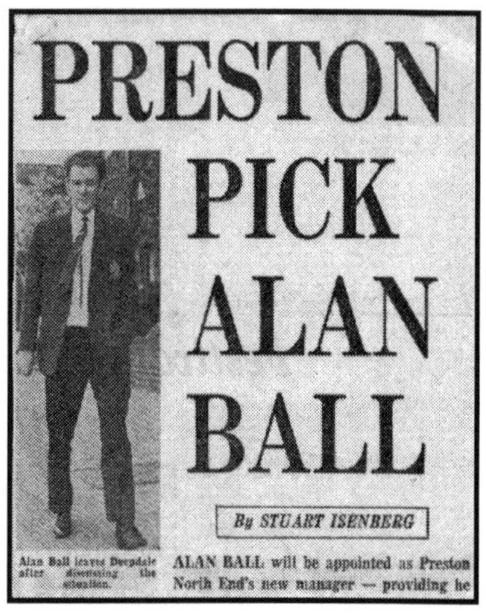

PRESTON PICK ALAN BALL

By STUART ISENBERG

Alan Ball leaves Deepdale after discussing the situation.

ALAN BALL will be appointed as Preston North End's new manager — providing he

Right : Front Page News! The PNE board select Alan Ball Senior to be their new manager....assuming of course permission was forthcoming from Halifax Town

Indeed the LEP had been quite forthright in its criticism of the club since the end of that awful 1969/70 season. A front page article at the end of April was very withering of the North End board.

The editorial boomed, *"And let there be no mincing of words, they bear by far the biggest responsibility of all for the plight of a once - great club whose grandeur and tradition has been blundered away by a long saga of ineptitude and failure."* Adding that the newspaper had been flooded with letters of support for its stance from the paying fans it continued, *"They - like us have been badly let down. The only people who have kept their heads in Deepdale's summer of the long knives are the board. Hardly surprising if you are in the privileged position of writing the script and starring in the show - you are probably going to be reluctant to write yourself out of it."*

Strong stuff, but the correct medicine as it turned out. The appointment of Ball at least showed some thought and imagination by a board now obviously wary of how the public now perceived them.

Along with a fresh start, Ball would bring publicity for the club with his sometimes outspoken comments and media presence.

Within a few days of returning from holiday he got down to business. "**WORK OR GET OUT SAYS BALL"** was the LEP headline under which he explained that anybody not buying into the new regime or putting the effort in, would be on their way. *"I've arrived with an open mind, have no favourites but hate slackers. Anybody not pulling their weight will be out."*

The outgoing and incoming managers would appear to have been chalk and cheese. I have read books and articles over the years by former players about both; Bobby Seith was very well respected by the players, and a decent chap.

Alan Ball Snr wasn't apparently always as nice; he could be blunt sometimes and straight to the point, but knew lower division football inside out and how to encourage. The players seemed to like him too. He had been set a task by the board to rip out the old and bring in the new, so perhaps to a few he was never going to be 'Mr. Popular.'

David Hughes, just a 'rookie' on the North End staff at the time, recalled much later in a LEP interview, "Bally's pre-season talk to us must have been the shortest in North End's history. He just said, *'You are going to win the Third Division championship this season lads, give me 100%'* – and that was it!"

With many of the current playing staff already under contract, it was imperative that Ball re-signed those out of contract who he knew would be able to do a job for him. He convinced Archie Gemmill to put pen to paper, but you wondered if, with several First Division clubs openly interested in him, North End would really stand in his way if an all round beneficial deal emerged. North End not only needed promotion, they also needed cash. Alex Spark, that midfield work horse, was in the process of getting married in Scotland but sent word back that he would sign on again upon return.

There were casualties though. Derek Temple, the ex Everton star was sold at a massive loss to Wigan Athletic and fringe player Alan Tinsley moved on to Bury. The combined total raised from those two sales was £8,000, which would prove a significant sum later in the year. So, in a small way at least, the rebuild had begun.

The summer of 1970 was also the year of the Mexico World Cup. It was certainly something to cling on to if you were suffering from the aforementioned 'Deepdale depression.'

A glorious few weeks of football that has arguably never been bettered made this the best summer ever for a football mad teenager. England had a team that was almost the same XI every time, and it was a shock when they lost. England fans today will never know such luxury - and we had actually won the trophy just 4 years previously!

The epic against Brazil is still regarded by many as 'the game' of the '70 tournament; the eventual exit at the hands of the West Germans, being the low point with England squandering a 2-0 lead. Add to that a great family holiday to Scotland with perfect weather, which was made even better when, with the help of a petrol station owner near our hotel, I completed my Esso World Cup Coin Collection!

Meanwhile, back at Deepdale; Ball's plan for a pre-season tour of Holland had been arranged...and then cancelled by the Dutch clubs - North End winger David Wilson was wanted by Southport - and the team eventually set off for the first of their pre-season friendlies, travelling to Dumfries to take on Queen of the South. This was to be followed by a home game against Liverpool, then away to Oldham Athletic and Blackburn Rovers.

The Liverpool game on August 4th attracted over 11,000 to Deepdale and the rather predictable result of 0-5 ensued. North End were shredded that day by Shankly's men, in every which way. I distinctly recall the speed and flow of their moves involving ex North Ender Peter Thompson. He left our defenders on their backsides time and again.

How good was he?! All this however did nothing to convince the diehard fans that any sort of impression would be made on the Division Three campaign - just a few short weeks away.

After three of the pre-season friendlies, North End were winless, but Ball pronounced himself happy with certain personnel, in particular Graham Hawkins, whose defending he described as magnificent. However, he had to field searching questions about his toothless attack. *"I know what the problems are but very confident that we can achieve our aims even though we have no money to spend at the moment."* The cynics were starting to forecast how long it would be before North End hit the rocks of Division Four. Nothing had really changed after all, it seemed to them.

By now, in addition to Arthur Cox, a 'work them hard' type coach, and Trainer Harry Hubbick, both who also made the jump from Halifax Town, Ball had recruited ex Manchester United star Denis Viollet to the coaching staff, and wasn't afraid to use this Old Trafford connection in an attempt to lure stalwart defender Shay Brennan to North End; the former Ireland international having been given a free transfer.

The proposed move hit snags from the start; Ball, (probably due to the board only willing to sanction the outright signing of a forward) could only offer Brennan a three month trial period. Brennan had made it clear that North End were the preferred choice of his potential suitors but the interest eventually waned on both sides, with Ball unable to offer any improvement on his opening offer.

It was now Monday, August 10th, less than a week away from the big kick off. North End checked in at Ewood for their last pre season outing. Predictably, North End went down 2-0 – still no goals to show for their efforts. However, reports of the game suggested that apart from the obvious goal scoring 'dead zone', the team had acquitted themselves quite well. Ball had experimented with the team formations, and this had resulted in a faster tempo to their play.

On Wednesday, the LEP back page led with the headline, **"BALL BIDS TO END THE GOAL FAMINE"**, the article stating that Ball was away following up his interest in a forward he wanted to bring to Deepdale.

The possible targets listed were Bury's George Jones, George Yardley of Tranmere and Bobby Ham of Bradford City. By Thursday, the situation had evolved to the point where apparently Ham was at Deepdale talking over personal terms. The clubs had agreed a fee plus player deal – North End could have Ham for £5000 plus reserve goalkeeper Gerry Stewart. The only problem with that was .... Stewart had apparently no inclination to move to Bradford City.

By the eve of the big kick off of 1970/71, the Ham/Stewart situation had still not been resolved and although Ham was asking for a little more time to consider everything, the encouraging news was that Gerry Stewart had travelled over to Bradford to discuss the situation with City manager Jimmy Wheeler.

So, despite last minute transfer scrambling, North End would begin the campaign with basically the same squad that propped up Division Two in April 1970, with the added bonus of now being proven to be completely toothless in front of goal after the pre season friendlies. All the hopeful summer talk from Ball and the board now seemed a little hollow. Was this a case of the same old contents in a different wrapping paper?

So, it was with trepidation that I put my jacket on to catch the twenty past two bus on August 15th 1970, jumping off at Skeffington Road. I was off to witness my once proud club at the lowest ever point in their long and distinguished history.

The half mile walk down 'Skeffy' (Skeffington) Road on match day enabled you to overhear opinions, and also get an indicator of potential crowd size. On that day, none of those were positive.... Grumble, grumble, moan, moan.

August

The Big Kick Off, Halifax Town, Stockport County, Torquay United, Bristol Rovers, Wrexham

The squad for the season opener against Halifax Town was announced by Ball on the eve of the game. The new manager went with:

Kelly, Ross, McNab, Spark, Hawkins, Lyall, Wilson, Gemmill, Irvine, Ingram, Heppolette, Clark and Spavin.

As already noted, to say it had a familiar ring about it was the understatement of the year! This was the team that had failed so miserably the season before. Even as a 13 year old at the time I remember thinking that any 'success plan' was based on nothing more than hope.

During the pre season the issue of nominating the captain was proving a dilemma for Ball. Ross, Hawkins and McNab had all been tried with none getting the immediate nod. However, at five minutes to three, as the teams ran out to the signature tune strains of "Margie", it was Graham Hawkins who led North End out. On reflection that was one of many pivotal decisions that Ball got spot on. Hawkins proved to be a natural leader of men, sitting slap bang in the heart of the defence barking out both instructions and chastisements to his team mates. Without question the team responded to him.

Just under 10,000 turned up for what was a turgid performance by both teams. It was goalless at half time and as I sipped some of that famous tea, 'Earl Town End' (often described by the discerning elder fan as *'dishwatter'*), served in those chewable polystyrene cups, I got to thinking that perhaps there would be better things to do on a Saturday afternoon....

Just after half time, it got even worse. Here we are at the lowest point, and we go 0-1 down at home...to those world beaters...Halifax Town! It was a steady stream of boos that accompanied North End back to position for the kick off. Ball was being lambasted too. Frustrated at this after all the hope, I decided to go home early and made my way towards the big exit gates but for some reason couldn't go through with leaving. I hung around and within a couple of minutes Ricky Heppolette shot home the equaliser in front of the Town End after some neat interplay with Willie Irvine. What a relief! Perhaps we would not be further disgraced after all! The game petered out as a draw, obviously Halifax being the happier of the teams. Based on what we had witnessed, this was going to be another long, horrible season.

North End's opening goal of the 1970/71 campaign, Ricky Heppolette drives home from close range

In those heady football days, there was no instant communication by mobile phone or internet - they had yet to be invented. However, you only had to wait until about quarter past six in the evening to be fully conversant with all the day's football matters.

The reassuring thump of the "*Football Post*" on the hallway carpet was something to be loved and cherished. Pink in colour and packed full of information and features, I would spend hours scanning this wonderful broadsheet. This particular edition led with the headline, "**POINT FOR PNE BUT 'POOL BEATEN**." You have to smile. Those sub editors always tried to lift the Prestonians suffering from 'Deepdale depression'!

By Monday evening, the LEP was assuring us that Bobby Ham would be a North End player by Tuesday, as Ball had managed to convince Gerry Stewart that the move to Valley Parade was in his interests. Certainly a good news story to counter the general numb feeling of the fans following Saturday's laboured draw.

In typical North End fashion, a last minute hitch arose in the transfer saga over player valuations and the deal that was 'certain to happen' 24 hours previously was now well and truly off.

North End's next tour of duty was a League Cup tie at Stockport County. I didn't witness this game but it was reported as one of those contests where the underdogs go down to ten men and then proceed to rally. Despite creating most of the chances, County couldn't find the net; North End successfully contaminating them with their 'illness.' Once that was done, it was a healthy again Willie Irvine who slotted home our second of the season to sneak us through to the next round. The LEP quite properly concluded, "*...unhappily, improvements are only coming inch by inch.*"

Long trips to the outposts of football have often spelt doom for North End. As it turned out, the long haul to South Devon to play Torquay United at Plainmoor in the League was no different. Despite grabbing an early lead with an out of the blue shot from Gerry Ingram, North End yet again contrived to waste a hatful of chances to secure the points, before graciously for their hosts, making enough defensive errors to concede three goals. At first glance, the result was another head shaker. However, after the match Torquay manager Allan Brown was quoted as saying his team were flattered.

"Preston's movement was superb, and had Irvine not hit the post after a flowing move when they were leading 1-0, the result could well have been different." At last, some independent praise of North End. Perhaps Ball had got something going at long last...his post match comments once again centred on missed chances. He certainly *was* shaking his head.

There was rumour of a post match dressing room spat between Ball and Irvine over missed chances; I just hoped Willie could get back to his best, because at this level he would be lethal. Just two games in and it seemed the pressure was beginning to tell...

Next up was a home League double – Bristol Rovers on the 29th of August and Wrexham on the 31st.

The 12 man squad announced on Friday was:

Kelly, Ross, McNab, Spark, Hawkins, Heppolette, Wilson, Hughes, Gemmill, Irvine, Ingram, Clark.

.... the suggestion being that either Wilson or Hughes would sit on the bench. Ball was at pains to deny press speculation that he was tracking Birmingham City's Tony Hateley to solve the lack of goals crisis. He said that the players were angry about losing at Torquay the previous weekend and, in typical belligerent Ball fashion, was *"confident of a win."* He needed to be. After two League games, North End stood fourth from bottom of Division Three.

It was a lovely sunny afternoon with around 1500 less paying spectators than were at the Halifax game. And after half an hour of tedious, suppressed play you could see exactly why. North End then responded to some management arm waving from the bench and the tempo was raised. David Hughes who had experienced little difficulty in repeatedly outpacing Rovers' full back Alex Munro, did so yet again, and drilled a hard low cross in across the box which clipped a defenders leg. As the ball ran free, Gerry Ingram swiveled and buried the ball into the back of the net, without pausing for breath. Half time arrived soon after, and

North End left the field for their orange and a cup of tea to polite applause for a change.

No sooner had the second half started it seemed, than we were cheering another Ingram goal, this time from a cross by the overlapping full back George Ross. How good was this! We were on our way at last!

Left : Preston North End's very own 'Captain Fantastic', Graham Hawkins, takes control of the North End defence against Bristol Rovers

That good feeling was reined in a little when that superb Rovers, (and later to become Aston Villa), winger Ray Graydon reduced the deficit back to one. He had been largely stifled by Jim McNab, but his quality eventually shone through with a neat finish.

It was finger nail chewing time. There was about 25 minutes left when Rovers' left sided midfielder Bryn Jones changed the game – and not in a good way. He was sent off for an appalling tackle on the North End dynamo, aka 'Go-Go' Gemmill, and North End would soon profit. In the 72nd minute it was Hughes again slinging yet another cross over inviting Willie Irvine to head home in glorious fashion from the inside right position. That should have been it, but it wasn't. The nerves returned with about ten minutes left, when from a corner, Phil Roberts rose high above a transfixed North End defence to bury a header in the corner of the net.

How sweet it was when that final whistle finally blew. We had won, and scored three goals! Let's not dwell too much on the two goals conceded; North End needed a break from criticism.

The walk back to the bus stop at the top of 'Skeffy Road' was very enjoyable, with much talk about North End's first win.

I was waiting, pacing up and down the hallway when the *Football Post* finally arrived. The headline read, **"PRESTON GAIN FIRST VICTORY"** along with a more favourable report than usual.

As the return to school loomed after such a great six week summer holiday, another North End home fixture was fitting compensation and just the tonic I needed to take away the feeling of dread that led in the pit of my stomach. It was present in me after every school holiday, no matter how long. The prospect of those ridiculous lessons of 'Modern Mathematics' – which I swear nobody understood – was too much to bear.

Wrexham were the visitors to Deepdale on what turned out to be a wet and wild Bank Holiday Monday night – in every sense.

The contest had just about everything. Both teams on all out attack; referee knocked out and stretchered off, torrential rain causing the match to be suspended, a glimpse of North End's new free kick invention, another five goals, and best of all....a North End win!

North End started the game with real pace and gusto, and the pay off was immediate. From a McNab free kick, Hughes crossed and Ingram headed in from close range. This domination fell off a little and a defensive error by McNab started a chain of events that led to Bob Park equalising for the Welshmen. With the North End sting extracted Wrexham went ahead before most of the crowd had returned to their places at the start of the second half; Kinsey the executioner.

If North End were sleeping they certainly woke up when the next event occurred. A full blooded Wrexham clearance caught the referee full on the back of the head, causing him to collapse in a heap on the floor. After the initial ironic cheering died down, it was obvious that Mr.

Leyden would be in no fit state to continue, so Linesman Mr. Wade assumed control after the stretcher left the pitch. An appeal for an emergency linesman resulted in local referee Mr. Nickson enjoying his half hour or so of glory running the Deepdale touchline for the remainder of the game.

The new ref awarded a free kick to North End on the edge of the penalty area and Wrexham formed the bog standard wall. However, what set off the crowd humming was when Irvine and Ingram muscled their way in to that wall too. Alex Spark ran in from a decent length and drove the ball straight at those two North Enders. Throwing themselves to the floor to leave a gaping hole in the wall, unbelievably the ball hit the back of the Wrexham net at some pace before the goalkeeper had even moved! There followed great celebrations from both crowd and players. Back in it - and in some style. That move was inspired by the Mexico World Cup, and we had pulled it off to perfection! Things like that just never happened at Deepdale...ever!

With the crowd roaring on this North End momentum swing, you could visibly see the confidence return to the team. Just a couple of minutes later, McNab hurtled down the left wing on an overlap. His low cross was met and stabbed in by Ingram in one complete movement on the run. The crowd noise was deafening as Ingram continued his run - around the back of the goals to be swamped by his team mates upon his return to the playing surface. This was absolutely superb fare, and North End were threatening even more before what can only be described as a monsoon descended over Deepdale.

So instantly intense was the rain that the referee had no option but to blow his whistle, grab the ball and motion to the players to head down the tunnel. An announcement to the crowd that the ref was hoping to continue 'as soon as it is possible' didn't dispel the murmurs in the home crowd that the game may well be abandoned. Fortunately, the game did resume after around 15 minutes, Hawkins ensuring that full points were collected with an injury time header off the North End goal line. Phew!

After the mini inquest as to why I was late getting home, "I've never heard of footballers going off for rain..." I reflected on the game for ages. It was a classic. Also becoming obvious was the influence of the 'Ball-isms' - they were certainly working. The free kick invention, the pace down the flanks, using Ingram as the main target - we certainly had something starting to go for us.

In fact Gerry Ingram's renaissance under the Ball regime had been astonishing. By the end of August he had a scored five League goals, compared to his previous season grand tally of just four.

North End stood lower mid table, while early pacemakers Fulham and Aston Villa led the table.

Above: Gerry Ingram celebrates the winner against Wrexham

September

Port Vale, Torquay United, Reading, Aston Villa, Bury, Fulham, Shrewsbury Town

Alan Ball must surely have identified September and October as key months in North End's first ever Division Three adventure. Twelve League games with 24 points at stake, a chance to establish a launching pad for the remainder of the season - not to mention two possible League Cup ties - as hopefully a victory over Torquay in the 2nd Round would take us into the draw with the big boys from Divisions One and Two.

The visit to Port Vale was the first hurdle. Vale, managed by a good but defensive minded coach, Gordon Lee (who would manage North End later in his career) promised to be stiff opposition. The wave of euphoria amongst the fans following Wrexham's defeat at Deepdale could well be short lived if North End were not on their mettle. Ball named an unchanged team chasing their third successive League win, Vale themselves having started with two wins and two losses.

The game was poor. North End had seemingly arrived at Vale Park in 'survive' mentality and it showed. They didn't survive. Offside traps and rugged tackling from Vale set the tone, the games' solitary goal coming from the penalty spot, after a cross was seemingly handled by George Ross. This is what North End had to expect from now on. They were a prized scalp from Division Two and teams would do all they could to prevent them producing performances such as those against Bristol Rovers and Wrexham.

Another long visit to Plainmoor was next on the fixture list. Having lost there a few weeks ago in the League, this time around it was a League Cup 2nd Round tie. Torquay manager, Allan Brown, generously penned in his programme notes, *"Make no mistake, Preston are a team that can get back into the Second Division."* Well, this being a cup tie, Ball and his men were more concerned with making the next round, hopefully drawing a top club and swelling that 'players wanted' fund.

Just as they got the Port Vale game all wrong, North End's performance at Plainmoor was absolutely 'spot on.' The 3-1 scoreline of a few weeks earlier was reversed, and the game hailed as a tactical triumph for Ball.

This time North End bided their time, playing football with a defensive emphasis. After sustaining an injury, Heppolette had to leave the field midway through the first half, leading to a major reorganisation in the North End midfield. Despite the odd scare around Kelly's goal, the plan was achieved - the half time whistle blowing with the score 0-0. After the break, North End upped the tempo. Brisk attacking moves caught the hosts on the hop, and before long North End went one up.

Shortly after having a shot cleared off the Torquay goal line, Wilson was fouled on the right wing. A quick free kick was taken, the ball crossed low some 20 yards out where it was met by Ingram. His first time shot flashed into the net via the post. And before too long, North End doubled their lead.

The dangerous Gemmill was fouled – on the edge of the penalty box. Indeed, the free kick taken by Spavin was just like a penalty. Hard hit and perfectly placed it left the keeper floundering as it arrowed home. It didn't stop there and in the 68th minute North End scored a third. It was a defensive mix up by a couple of home defenders which allowed the ball to break free to Ingram who fired home a shot without hesitation.

Despite a late rally in which Torquay scored their consolation goal,

North End had done their fans proud.

Who would we get in Thursdays draw? The banner headline in the Evening Post that night gave us the answer.

"NORTH END PLAY HOSTS TO ALBION." Excellent! A top tier side, (and the previous season's finalists), at Deepdale with household names like Astle, Suggett, Brown and Hartford in their team would be a great test of exactly where North End were in terms of performance, after their recent burst of good form.

Meanwhile Reading were on the Division Three horizon, and would grace the Deepdale turf on Saturday, September 12th. As the sun's rays beat down at Deepdale around five to three, the North End team was related to the crowd through that ancient ear piercing tannoy system:

Kelly, Ross, McNab, Spark, Hawkins, Spavin, Wilson, Gemmill, Ingram, Irvine and Lee. Sub Lyall

The vinyl with the familiar signature tune of 'Margie' was then thrown on to the record deck, and before you knew it both teams had completed their kick-in and North End were ready to kick off towards the Town End.

There were early exchanges from both teams, but North End were looking very nice on the eye. With good use of the wings, and Spavin and Gemmill dominating the midfield – what could possibly go wrong? Nothing really!

After 24 minutes, the Lilywhites went one up. As opponents were now finding, to stop the 'North End Goal Machine' Ingram, they had to cut off the endless supply of crosses from the two North End wingers of the day. This time it was Wilson who was hacked down after waltzing around the outside of the Reading left half. Spavin walked over to take the free kick. Ingram timed his run from the penalty spot to the front post perfectly to meet the floating ball and buried it from close range.

It was noticeable how different the chatter was on the terraces these days. Instead of moan first, and moan again later, it was encouragement and applause as it was gradually becoming visible what Ball was trying to achieve.

No more visible than on 29 minutes when Ingram put yet another into the back of the Reading net. After Wilson had yet again beaten his marker, he crossed low for Irvine to collect the ball. Under challenge, he passed the ball back to the oncoming Ingram who coolly slotted it past Steve D'eath in the Reading goal. Irvine almost took North End to three up just before half time. A through ball from Ingram to Wilson as North End broke just over half way, was fed into the arriving Irvine from the by line, but he shot over on the turn from about five yards out.

A magnificent half of North End football saw them applauded off with the chants of 'Alan Ball, Alan Ball' ringing around the ground.

No sooner had I finished my half time 'dishwatter' from the kiosk, than North End scored a third following a goalmouth scramble. A Gemmill free kick was floated in for Ingram to attack and his header was parried by the keeper. Ingram then tried a shot, but again the keeper blocked it, the ball running out to around the penalty spot from where Wilson drove the ball home through the melee.

Wilson, the former England Under 23 International was having a great game. There is no finer sight than a winger demonstrating his skill and craft to an appreciative crowd. This was certainly one of those days.

The game was rapidly becoming a stage for the North End players to showcase exactly what they were about this particular season. Any potential Reading raid was being snuffed out, the North End defence completely at ease. A superb spontaneous bicycle kick by Irvine almost pulled off an unlikely fourth for North End, but D'eath eventually saved after a defender headed back to him from the goal line.

After Spavin brought the house down with a mazy run, beating two players and slamming in a shot on goal, the super-charged Gemmill went one better! Embarking on a typical fast run he amazingly *dummied* his way past three defenders on the hoof and nonchalantly laid the ball off into the path of the supporting Ingram's left foot. The swing of that left foot transferred the ball to the back of the Reading net in an instant. Delighted North End fans went crazy after that wonderful passage of play.

It was the next rare Reading venture into North End's half that saw them reduce the deficit back to three. A foul by McNab in the box on attacker Dick Habbin enabled Gordon Cumming to slot home past Kelly from the penalty spot.

Using a reverse psychology technique, Ball - while professing himself pleased with the win – wanted more. More goal chances converted; more stability at the back. He added it was no good being satisfied with a few wins, if the team were just not improving on their weaknesses. Still, the fans were a lot happier, myself included. The talk at school at this time was all about North End winning their games – a habit that they had completely lost over previous seasons.

The spectacular Willie Irvine overhead kick against Reading at Deepdale

A rare week followed, with no midweek game to worry about. Good job really - as next up was an away fixture at Villa Park.

Pacesetters Villa sat third in the table, with 8 points from 6 games, just a point behind Bradford City, and a further point behind Fulham. Out of interest, North End sat ninth, with just one point fewer than Villa. Villa's lowest home crowd to date had been for the visit of Doncaster Rovers, when a 'trifling' 23,000 had turned up. North End hadn't got a great history in dealing well with these big away fixtures – in my time watching them anyway – so part of me was saying don't expect too much....

I was right to be sceptical. For some reason I can't recall, (no details to jog my memory in my scrapbook), I couldn't follow this game, but had no doubt seen the final score come through on the BBC Grandstand teleprinter.

Once through the letter box and unfolded, the Saturday *Football Post* led with the headline, **"LOCHHEAD DESTROYS NORTH END."** In a piece called *'The North End Verdict'* the Evening Post's North End correspondent, Norman Shakeshaft, related the tale of woe. Villa were obviously a class above...North End were caught on the hop...Villa dominated throughout...as did ex North Ender Brian Godfrey...North End were simply second best.

The negative comments throughout the piece appeared justified. Ball somehow had to rid the team of this habit of freezing in the headlights like shivering rabbits in games played in front of large crowds – in this case over 26,000. Going behind after just two minutes set the tone for the game; in the end conceding just two goals was probably a miracle.

By Monday, Ball was playing the reverse psychology card again. After the great display against Reading the previous week, he had attempted to keep his players feet well and truly on the floor by saying improvements were still needed. After the tame defeat at Villa, Ball was cuddling his players. Agreeing that Villa were the best side North End had faced this season, he pointed out that it was far too early to consider them a cert for promotion. *"Let's see how they go on at places like Halifax in the depths of winter in front of a couple of thousand on a terrible pitch,"* was his response to the press comparison of the two teams.

North End had an away fixture at Bury on Tuesday, but it was on the way home on the school bus that some very sad news broke. The conductor told a few of us the he had read in the Evening Post that Archie Gemmill had been transferred to Derby County. The sick feeling in the pit of my stomach wasn't helped when I finally raced down the hallway when the LEP fell through the letterbox.

"GEMMILL MOVES TO COUNTY FOR £70,000," the headline read. Along with pictures of a smug looking Brian Clough and a smiling Archie Gemmill, there it all was; signed, sealed and delivered. The story suggested that Clough had obviously received information that Everton were about to bid for Gemmill, a player he said he had watched several times. Clough had travelled up to Preston on Monday with sidekick Peter Taylor and Stuart Webb (the former PNE Club Secretary), to spend personal time with his target, after receiving permission to do so from the North End board.

Although that isn't incorrect, it was the only part of the piece that was vaguely accurate. The 'warts and all' story has since come to light about Gemmill's North End experiences, in his autobiography.

It would appear that after Archie bluntly asked for - and received - a well deserved wage rise at the start of the season, the North End board had apparently been happy for Ball to openly tout Gemmill to his close friend Harry Catterick and even the Everton players via his son, and a deal was all but done with the Merseyside club.

Indeed, Gemmill had apparently discussed the move to Everton with both his family and Catterick and was all set to move clubs within days, thinking the call to come into Deepdale on Sunday morning was to be the transfer signing session. It wasn't - it was to be personally informed by Ball that Mr. Clough was coming to see him the following day...and the rest is history.

At first glance, even now, I still wonder about the seemingly low fee that North End let Gemmill go for.

So did the North End board undervalue their prized asset?

The answer, as always, is it depends on which view you take....

Bearing in mind that this transfer took place 45 years ago, to nail this once and for all, I visited The Bank of England online UK Inflation Converter to enter the 1970 transfer fee of £70,000 and see exactly what the computer spat out as today's value. The record fee back then stood at £200,000 for World Cup winner Martin Peters.

In fact, after factoring in inflation, Archie 'Go-Go' Gemmill was sold for the equivalent today of £969,134. Add to that the fact he hadn't become widely famous by then, and also with North End more than likely not wanting a potentially disaffected player on their books – and it maybe wasn't so bad a deal for a club placed mid table in Division Three with cash flow problems.

The 'Gemmill Saga' apart, North End had a chance to redeem themselves after the insipid performance at Villa Park the previous Saturday. They were visiting Gigg Lane to take on Bury with Ricky Heppolette assigned to take over the departed Gemmill's role. North End fielded:

Kelly, Ross, McNab, Spark, Hawkins, Spavin, Wilson, Irvine, Ingram, Heppolette, Hughes. Sub Lyall

The outcome was just the tonic needed. Described as a busy and workmanlike display, North End brought home the bacon after a solitary Ingram goal settled the issue. The big news was that so good was Heppolette in his new role, the pundits were already saying North End could probably manage without 'Go-Go' as the season went forward.

That was good to hear, as was the description of skipper Graham Hawkins performance by Ball as, *"tremendous."*

Pick of the forwards was the ebullient Ingram who, running onto a through pass from partner Willie Irvine, slid the ball under the advancing keeper and into the back of the net. His tally for the season now stood at 11, exceeding his first team aggregate for the two previous seasons. He was given excellent support throughout by the wingers once again, Hughes and Wilson, the latter always a danger to the Bury defence. A 1-0 lead away from home will always need some closing out, but North End managed this too, despite a late Bury rally.

The pre-Vilia buzz was certainly back in North Ends play, with refreshing sharpness and aggression on display. The hope was that this would continue as North End hosted runaway League leaders Fulham at Deepdale on the coming Saturday....

Friday night's LEP provided the team news. Frank Lee was on standby for left flank duties should David Hughes fail a Saturday morning fitness test. Otherwise it was the same team that had 'got back on the horse' at Bury.

There was a good deal of excitement at school about this game and a couple of us decided to meet up outside the West Stand before the game. Official programmes firmly in hand, we decided to stump up the extra 'tanner' and pay 3/- (that's 15p for post decimalisation babies), and watch from the West Paddock. This would enable us to see North End attack each goal by wandering to the other end of the Paddock at half time.

Time to revisit the online UK Inflation Converter to see just how much in today's terms we were paying as juveniles to watch vintage North End! Just £2.20 per game! Bargain!!

I have some vivid memories of this game. Fulham were resplendent in light and dark blue striped shirts which seemed quite 'arty' for the time. North End, kicking towards the Town End, made all the first half running. In an enterprising and fast paced first half they came near to scoring on three occasions; early in the game through Ingram, after around half an hour through Wilson and closest of all via Heppolette, whose diving header hit the post. Fulham's noted attackers had gone AWOL during this dominant North End display.

Off we trundled to get down to the Kop end of the West Paddock, gingerly skipping past an official when his back was turned who discouraged such activity from his half way line posting. There was time enough to check the half time score boards that were placed on both sides of the ground. The selected games each had a letter and a score, the key to the teams involved being found at the back of the programme. Letter 'Q', 1-1. That was West Brom v Derby County. Had Archie scored on his First Division debut?

Meanwhile, at Deepdale Ricky Heppolette's new verve was convincing the fans that we could well have a new star in the making.

How unfair can football be? Having completely outplayed Fulham in the first half, the second period was only minutes old when the Londoners took a very streaky and fortuitous lead. From a right wing corner, a shot came swinging in, rebounded off a North End defender....straight into the path of John Richardson who drilled the ball home without any hesitation.

I distinctly remember my pal saying, "Here we go..." and myself feeling gutted that all the enterprising play so far had come to naught.

But this was to be a milestone day – when North End realised that they were Fulham's - and for that matter anybody else's - equals or betters. Instead of defaulting to 1969/70 mode, as at Villa Park, they grasped the game by the scruff of the neck and forced a quite stunning equaliser.

That most reliable, and 'key' right back George Ross, saw the initial opening. Pelting forward down the right wing leaving two retreating Fulham players in his wake, he teamed up with fellow full back Jim McNab, chipping the ball across field into his path. By the time McNab had returned the ball yet again and made his way into the box, he was in position to power home a quite stunning header from the resulting cross. It was a classic leap - McNab's coiling body meeting the ball in a powerful forward motion. The Fulham defence were transformed into mere statues.

Everybody was jumping up and down! We were exactly in line to see the header executed too. Marvelous stuff!!!

The game became more even after that, North End having no real problems in dealing with the renowned Fulham forward line, whist creating the odd bit of pressure themselves. What a pity we couldn't force the win.

Watched by a crowd of over 12,000 this was my game of the season so far, even eclipsing the Wrexham game. North End had looked every bit as good, if not better than Fulham - who were top of the pile. At long last, perhaps the team were getting in tune with what Ball was demanding, and of what the fans expected of them.

Jim McNab powers home a header to equalise against Fulham

North End's final League outing of this fixture packed month was away at Shrewsbury Town, fittingly on the last day of September. Shrewsbury sat ninth - just above North End in the table, but a check on their fixture list showed that so far they had mainly played teams below them. They had, however bagged 19 goals, making them one of the Divisions most potent attacks.

Ball decided to move Willie Irvine to the substitute's bench, and start with Frank Lee. This would prove to be inspired thinking.

North End started well, threatening danger early on. Hughes featured in the first two attempts, which were blocked en route to goal, but it wasn't long before North End struck. Ingram, with his back to goal, shielded the ball and turned it out to Wilson on the right. As was commonly happening nowadays, Wilson left his marker standing taking the ball to the byline before turning it back into the path of Hughes, whose shot was once again blocked. This time the ball ran free to the incoming Heppolette who crashed an unforgiving shot into the roof of the net from around the six yard box. Much joy all round!

The 'Shrews,' as one would imagine lifted their game and forged a couple of decent chances themselves, the best of which saw McNab block a great drive by Dave Roberts. Much to the away fans delight though, it was North End who kept creating the best chances, in particular a superb free kick from the edge of the box from Spavin that just clipped the home bar.

The second half captured in a nutshell how things were evolving at North End, in terms of managerial doctrine and player attitude. Twelve months previously, North End would have been petrified if they were leading 1-0 away from home at half time; totally devoid of ideas and ability to see the game out.

This season was different. They set about Shrewsbury in the second half much as they had in the first. Sporadic raids by the home team were as good as it got for them, while North End continued to pile in the chances. Ingram was upended just outside the box while rounding a defender, Heppolette headed a fraction wide, a defender almost turned a Wilson cross into his own net, and another effort by the flying winger was saved at full stretch by the keeper.

This increased second half pressure on the Shrewsbury goal was panicking the home defence into poor clearances, the ball being returned with interest by a rampant North End. Wilson hammered a shot into the side netting, Spavin once again shaved the bar with a superb shot from the edge of the box and Lee had a header frantically saved by the keeper. With their 100% home record slipping away, the 'Shrews' fired their last salvo just before the end, Alan Kelly snuffing out the only real danger, diving at the feet of Terry Harkin when there was half a chance the winger would score.

And what of Frank Lee's performance?

Ball inventively gave the North End veteran a free role when naming him instead of Irvine in the starting lineup. He was everywhere bar his usual place on the flank. Midfield, defence, attack – he was tackling, supporting and initiating North End movement around the pitch. It was an inspiring performance from this loyal soldier.

Another two points in the bag; how great it was that North End were actually *winning* away matches! The ever improving North End now stood sixth in Division Three, with 12 points from their ten games. Since the Villa debacle, they had taken five points from a possible six, including two away wins. A lesson had certainly been learned that day at Villa Park.

Ball's ability to get the best out of the very same players who had been so abject the season before was startling. Add to the mix the obvious belief of the players in their manager - and also themselves – and you had a club heading in the right direction. Make no mistake, if things had been left as they were, it would have been the basement beckoning North End.

Last, but not least, in a post match interview Ball mentioned for the first time, 'The Gentry.' These were enthusiastic fans, turning up in their hundreds at away venues North End had never visited before, shouting loud and proud for the team who were giving them new found hope.

Ball's famous words cemented the bond between fans and the new manager, *"It's great to see these people travelling as far as Shrewsbury for a night match. To see youngsters clapping and cheering behind the goal is terrific. Some people may call them hooligans. As far as I'm concerned, they are the Gentry."*

Today, 45 years on, the Gentry still survive. Ball's camaraderie with the fans lives on in spirit. Indeed, a great story reported at the time encapsulates just what the whole Gentry phenomena meant to both manager and fan.

As the North End team coach drew up outside Home Park, Plymouth in October 1970, the Gentry were all in position. As the players stepped off, they were greeted with a tremendous roar...and then came Alan Ball.

With a solemn face, he stood still and waved his arm as if conducting an orchestra with a baton and, in total unison, the Bowler bedecked Gentry were silenced, and bowed forward in allegiance! Absolute loyalty!!

Alan Ball, creator of the Gentry addressing a fans meeting in 1970/71, showing them how it's done by donning his Bowler

The Gentry lives on. Special 'Gentry Days' are still arranged for the travelling fans to enjoy. Today they are used to commemorate the passing of fans or players during the past year...

October

Bradford City, League Cup Exit, Mansfield Town, Transfer Speculation, Halifax Town, Swansea City, Plymouth Argyle, Brighton & Hove Albion

The first week of the new month was going to be busy. North End had a tricky away fixture at Valley Parade on Saturday, 3rd October, followed by a League Cup tie against West Bromwich Albion at home on the following Wednesday.

Ball decided to name the same squad that had smashed Shrewsbury Town's 100% home record a few days earlier. Interestingly, the LEP noted that Bobby Ham would be in the Bradford City team; Preston's failure to secure his signature earlier in the season being Ball's major regret to date.

Before kick off, Frank Lee who had played so well at Shrewsbury had to withdraw due to stomach trouble. In came Willie Irvine, who every North End fan was hoping would rediscover his goal scoring touch.

North End, as was their style these days, dominated the first half completely. City looked all at sea, with Spavin controlling the centre of the pitch, and the rapid pace of Wilson and Hughes pinning the defence back time and again. Indeed, Wilson was giving the City full back Ian Cooper a torrid time, at one stage turning him one way then the other, before the hapless backpedaling defender fell on all fours.

Two corners were won by Wilson in quick succession. The second of these caused some consternation in the City goalmouth before the ball was cleared straight into the path of the rampaging Ingram, whose powerful shot was superbly turned round the post by keeper, Pat Liney.

A goal was certainly coming....and when it did it was a cracker.

Following excellent approach work between Heppolette and Irvine, Wilson received a pass on the right before cutting infield and precisely placing a shot into the corner of the City net.

City, under vocal pressure from their fans, tried to rally, but the half ended with North End leading deservedly.

The second half started as the first had ended, with North End saying how it was going to be. It was around the hour mark when North End doubled their lead, a Spavin centre reaching the back of the net with a thump via the head of Gerry Ingram. The bowed heads of the City defence as they made their way back to their positions for the kick off must have struck a sympathetic chord with North End, as there is no doubt that from this point there was an easing off in their intensity.

This allowed City to emerge from under the rocks a little and attempt to salvage some reward. However, even in 'relaxed' mode, North End managed to keep a clean sheet by the time the final whistle blew. By the way, Bobby Ham, the pre-season North End transfer target, was also kept quiet.

Two more points in the bag, now seven from a possible eight in the last four games. You would think the manager would be pleased! It was reverse psychology time again....

"Yes, I know we won 2-0 but we relaxed and became casual after scoring the second – this I do not want! I told the lads off at the end, and insisted they keep driving forward for the full 90 minutes."

For the fans though, it was just magnificent! Personally, I could not recall North End winning three away games in a row - just like my friends at school. North End were the talk of the playground these days rather than United, City, Liverpool or Everton.

Their popularity was breeding a new type of teenager follower. The corporation bus poster snatcher!

A few days before each home game, there had for years been the practice of a small but perfectly formed window bill poster being tacked to one of the downstairs windows of corporation buses. It was usually a window near the back platform of the buses, where the conductor hung about. I had begun to notice that by the day after these posters had made their 'debut' there was an empty gap with five glue marks left on the glass.

This never used to happen, what was going on?

One day after school, I actually admiring one of these increasingly rare mini posters on the school bus going into town, when the conductor went upstairs to collect his fares. As soon as he was out of sight three lads leapt toward the poster, the first one there expertly prising the poster off the glass, rolling it up and stuffing it into his school bag in the blink of an eye. The others just returned to their seats and said nothing. The conductor never even noticed when he returned.

At the bus station I asked the snatcher what it was all about. He replied he was "going for the full set this season" but was "missing the Halifax game"....!

It got me to thinking. They *were* quite unique - and I did collect North End bits and pieces already.

As it was, there was a regular driver and conductor team to our terminus on the standard public service. One day soon after, deliberately leaving the bus last, I plucked up enough courage to ask the conductor if I could take the North End poster from the window just behind him. He could only say, *'hoppit kid'* or similar couldn't he?

Sounding tired, his answer was just what I wanted to hear. *"You might as well, every other bugger does!"*

Meanwhile, North End were taken to Morecambe sands to tweak their fitness in readiness for the visit of West Bromwich Albion in the League Cup third round tie. It became obvious that Ball desperately wanted to impress the footballing world by taking the scalp of the First Division outfit, which had star quality within their ranks.

A crowd of over 18,000 filled Deepdale, many hoping for a similar outcome as Ball. Indeed it was North End who played all the football in the first half, lifting the expectation that they could well see off Albion and progress even further in the competition.

Around the ten minute mark, Hughes, Spavin and Wilson combined to force a corner on the right. Menacingly placed by Wilson, Heppolette's lunge at the ball resulted in a hurried clearance back in the winger's direction, who promptly hammered back a shot into the danger zone. As the ball bounced around, Ingram then moved forward to shoot towards goal, but Jim Cumbes, the cricketing goalkeeper, expertly smothered the effort.

Ingram and Irvine then combined to put unexpected pressure on the Albion centre backs, resulting in a desperate punt away to clear the ball. The crowd was certainly roaring North End on, and Albion looked distinctly uncomfortable.

It wasn't until after the half hour mark that Albion really poked their noses out past the half way line. In a mini period of domination, a swerving free kick by Bobby Hope, a volley by England World Cup striker Jeff Astle and a sliced Colin Suggett shot tested North End's powers of concentration. The half closed with a great appreciation from the home crowd ringing in North End's ears, but Ingram seemed to be limping as the trudged towards the tunnel....

Ingram returned to the battlefield with his leg strapped for the second half, and obviously buoyed by Ball's half time words, the home team set the pace again. A right wing run by Wilson saw him seemingly transfix the Albion defence as he carved out an opening to cross for Ingram whose effort to get a decent header on target was obviously hampered by his leg injury. After a further chance had fallen to North End's leading scorer in which he struggled to connect, he was replaced by Clive Clark, the ex-Albion winger.

However, as always seems to happen, it was the opposition who took the lead; it must be said well against the run of play. Losing the attention for once of his marker Spavin, Asa Hartford drove the ball home after a delightful chip from the classy Tony Brown. This brought a spring to the step in Albion's play and they started to close North End out.

That prompted Ball to leave the dugout and pace up and down the touchline urging his players on. The crowd welcomed such input and roared on the home team in tune with Ball's arm waving. How badly Ball wanted that win that would give North End much needed credence! It prompted a gallant last ditch assault on the Albion goal.

A thunderbolt shot, just a fraction too high by John MacMahon, standing in for the injured McNab, set off ten minutes of breathtaking action. An Irvine header was desperately hacked away, and a dribble from the back and cross by Hawkins had Clark heading just over the bar.

Finally, it was over. It's fair to say that League Cup specialists Albion will rarely have had such a severe examination. For Ball though, it was a great disappointment. Despite plaudits and back slapping regarding North End's display from fellow managers present at the game, he was desolate.

"The point is that we lost and losers get nothing. This was our big chance to prove to the soccer public that we really are on the way back and we missed out. Praise is all very well but millions will hear the bare result on TV and radio and it conveys Preston were beaten. This is not good for the club."

While Ball was forgetting all about the team's superb effort and concentrating on the actual result, not many of the home fans were too disappointed. How refreshing to see a manager actively willing his players on, getting involved and be so downbeat to lose.

Personally, I thought that considering Albion were the previous seasons finalists, we gave them a fright. Yes, we lost but I didn't mind losing if the effort was there. Any signs of giving up as in the previous years had been banished. We were definitely witnessing a Deepdale upswing; a revival.

Friday's LEP back page led with **"INGRAM RULED OUT – LEE BACK"** - not news that the fans wanted to see or hear after the monumental effort in midweek against Albion. Apparently Ingram's injury, sustained in that game had not had time to recover. Lee's last outing had won rave reviews, so no worries there - but a reshuffle up front would be necessary. Mansfield Town were the visitors, they held 14 points, as did North End, but they had a game in hand on the Lilywhites.

By the time the North End tannoy crackled into action on Saturday afternoon, Ball had opted to give Irvine another opportunity up front, introducing reserve forward Norman 'Norrie' Lloyd to the first team scene on the subs bench.

North End began brightly, passing and moving briskly. It wasn't long - two minutes in fact - before we were all jumping up and down, celebrating the opening goal. Hughes, having forced a corner wide on the left, was rewarded with a second go when the panicking 'Stags' defence hoofed his cross back into touch rather than have the approaching Irvine getting interested. Hughes whipped in his next corner and Heppolette, running towards goal and in open space met it perfectly and headed the ball home. A fantastic start.

By the 19th minute, it was happiness again - the crowd once more going wild as Heppolette repeated the medicine, running into a wide open space in the box and picking his bottom corner spot with some aplomb.

There then followed complete North End control and dominance, with Spavin controlling the midfield, bringing the wingers Wilson and Hughes into play wherever possible.

At half time, the talk was all about the Albion game a few days before NOT being a fluke in terms of effort and performance, this first half display apparently proving the point. However, while North End were never in any real danger of losing this match, the second half was a little drab in comparison. It was when John Stenson nipped in and scored for the visitors, that the home crowd strangely sort of 'turned' on North End and started booing and slow handclapping them, as they appeared to withdraw into a 'pre Ball era' shell.

Ball's instructions were an attempted exercise in 'keep ball' by North End, and we just about made it over the finish line. Ball's last quarter tactics certainly had the fans talking on the way home - what on earth had all that been rubbish been about? On a positive note, North End were now fourth in the table, with nine points out of the last ten safely banked – so surely we shouldn't complain too loudly?

It was left to Alan Spavin to explain the goings on in Monday's LEP. Under the title of **"RICKY A REVELATION,"** Spavin roundly endorsed Ball's tactics by explaining that the superhuman effort against West Brom during the week had sapped a lot of energy from the team fuel tank and they were jaded well before the end of the Mansfield game. Ball added he was far from disheartened and, *"...we did well to hang on as several of my players were extremely tired."*

With no 'transfer windows' back in the 70's, speculation about player moves was season long – well until the March deadline day at least. So, after his recent performances it was only natural to groan out loud when the Tuesday's edition of the LEP was opened.

"TOP CLUBS LINE UP FOR RICKY" was the banner headline, along with an inset isolated quote from Ball, *"We do not know what types of deals and propositions will be put forward to us in the future and I can tell you now that anyone in my team can go for ...£75,000."*

In the article Ball did not deny that the Blackpool scout had spoken to him after Saturday's game but was at pains to say that Heppolette had

NOT been the subject of their conversation.

He qualified his 'anyone can go' quote by saying that every player everywhere has a price, and North End were a business after all – but he certainly didn't want any of them to leave.

Everton, the club who had missed out on our one player so far who did 'have a price,' were reported to have sealed a deal with Nottingham Forest to sign their midfielder Henry Newton for £150,000 – over twice the North End asking price for Archie Gemmill...

During the previous fortnight, Ball had employed the services of Peter Doherty, a very famous player of the past, to help create a back room support service for him, amongst other things keeping tabs on possible transfer targets.

The depressing article thus ended with the slightly upbeat news that while Doherty had watched future opponents Swansea City at the weekend, he had also run the rule over Bobby Ham once more playing for Bradford City in the same game.

The question that was on every North End followers lips on Friday and Saturday was, 'Would Ball manage to pull off a win at his old club Halifax and stretch North End's fine run a little further?'

Disappointingly, it was a no.

On what the press described as a 'ploughed field,' Halifax scraped the win with a single goal – a freak of a free kick that the referee controversially allowed Halifax to retake.

North End started brightly enough but couldn't express themselves on the poor surface and Ball, having warned his players beforehand about the 'agricultural land' and the 'depressing stadium' was quick to defend his beaten warriors after the game with his trusty psychology - this time the upbeat version reserved for defeats.

"I have a great side and it will become greater, but that doesn't mean to

say we can play our best on a cabbage patch," he declared at the post match press conference.

As the North End coach headed back home with the players happy to take Ball's advice to 'forget all about this one' they found that actually they literally had. They had left Frank Lee and Gerry Ingram behind at The Shay!

Ah well, time to drop North End down the table a couple of places on my 'Shoot' magazine League Ladder as Bristol Rovers and Mansfield muscle in above us. Let's hope for better on Monday night, when we take on Swansea City at Deepdale.

"Absolutely brilliant!" or something along those lines, were the words I probably shouted as I scanned the most important page in the LEP – the sports page.

"BALL GETS HIS MAN: HAM AGREES TO SIGN" said the headline, followed by full details of the deal. Ham was at Deepdale signing that very afternoon. The fee was £8,000 – the very same figure that North End gleaned from the sale of Derek Temple and Alan Tinsley way back in early August. This seemed a very fair swap for the cash that had been burning a huge hole in Ball's pocket.

The article moved onto the team news for the Swansea game that night, reporting that Jim McNab would still be marked as absent, and would now be joined by the speedy David Hughes, struck down with a heavy cold. In came Clive Clark and Norman Lloyd to cover. Ham of course was ineligible, with 48 hours clearance needed after putting pen to paper.

With North End hoping to climb back on the horse with a home win, this was to be one of those frustrating evenings where they did everything right except grab the two points. Indeed, from the 30th minute when Barrie Hole hammered a shot past Kelly, it looked as if they weren't even going to glean even a draw despite their very best efforts.

From the outset North End attacked the Swansea goal from every conceivable angle; crosses, headers and shots raining in on David Davies between the Swansea sticks. The youngster acquitted himself very well on many occasions in what was a fine display.

After half time, North End continued to press even harder, this strategy leaving the 'back door' open at times enabling fast, threatening breaks by the visitors – Dave Gwyther and Len Hill in particular testing Kelly to the limit. To go further behind would have been a great injustice, with North End completely dominating the game. Chance after chance was spurned, Heppolette, Spavin and the outstanding Clark all disappointing with their final touch.

Bobby Ham finally signs on the dotted line; this was a significant turning point in North End's season....

You always knew when there was around ten minutes left at Deepdale as the crowd would gently start leaving as the gates were unlocked. Not this time! With the 10,000 plus crowd cheering on the North End onslaught, Ball threw his last roll of the dice. He brought on Irvine to replace young Lloyd, who had been very impressive alongside Ingram.

With just minutes left, Clark sped past his marker and curled in a typical cross on the run to catch Ingram in space and Davies out of position. Ingram buried the header to notch his 13th goal of the season.

As the ball flew into the vacant net, the silence was deafening for a split second as the crowd almost wanted to make sure we had actually scored. Then it was the noise that was deafening. From my vantage point on the West Paddock close to the Kop, it was a superbly executed move. The goal provided much joy for the players too, much running around and hugging, while even that calmest of players, George Ross, supporting Ingram in the box, followed in and rammed the ball back into the net just for good measure, getting himself tangled up in the process.

So, only a solitary point to show from a possible four, but such an encouraging display. Ball 'bigged up' his team in the post match press conference. *"They made four chances, we made 400,"* was his simple analysis. Not quite, but they all knew what he meant.

Bobby Ham was in the stands watching his new team mates. He saw no reason why North End wouldn't do well going forward. Keen to pair up with Ingram, he said *"I have had to play in midfield lately with Bradford, but I'm keen to get back up front with North End."*

The LEP back page on Tuesday was as desperate as Monday's had been hopeful. Dwarfing the Swansea match report was a big story, all banner headlines, capitals and bold print.

"RICKY: RUMOURS GROW" it shouted. Apparently Blackpool and West Bromwich Albion representatives had been at Deepdale the night before to specifically watch the young midfielder turn in yet another classy display. To be fair, Heppy had come into his own since the departure of Archie Gemmill, relishing replicating his old mate's role in midfield.

The Blackpool directors were thought to be going to offer either centre forward Fred Pickering or Ronnie Brown (his reserve deputy) plus cash. Maybe if they had done this a little earlier Ball could have been interested - but surely having now signed Ham there was no need for either of the Blackpool players to be added to the North End squad. I suppose we would have to wait and see - but one thing was for sure; our players were now being noticed by all and sundry.

The long trek to Home Park, Plymouth beckoned next, the sixth game of a busy October. The Argyle coach, Bryan Edwards promised a special effort from his players for the visit of North End - his former employer. This was effectively waved aside by Ball in his pre match press conference, advising Edwards that he should really concentrate on every team, not just Preston. *"We go into all games looking for two points. So should he,"* was the advice.

With young John McMahon deputising at left back for a third time for the injured McNab, Irvine was nominated to make way in the squad for Ham, the only other decision for Ball was to perm two out of three from Wilson, Clark and Lee. In the event, it was Wilson and Clark who were named as starters, Lee keeping the bench warm.

In front of a crowd approaching 10,000, North End, as was their style set off briskly, but Argyle were spirited enough to exchange almost tit for tat any North End salvos.

The game developed nicely, and either side could claim to be unlucky not to lead. A great turn and shot by Shepherd rattled North End's post with Kelly well beaten, but at the other end, debut boy Ham should really have opened his account for the Lilywhites, but his miscued shot was eventually scrambled off the line by Pat Dunne, the keeper. Clark was busy for North End down the left wing, causing trouble for the home team as the North End midfield funneled the attack through him. As the game moved towards half time Argyle ramped up the pressure but despite a couple of shots being saved by Kelly, the North End defence stood firm under the reassuring guidance of Hawkins.

The second half opened with North End still buzzing around in midfield with Spavin pulling the strings. It took just seven minutes from the kick off for Ham to have the honour of scoring on his North End debut - and what a strike it was! Moving forward towards the Plymouth goal, he let fly on the run from around 20 yards, the pile driver curling away from the airborne Dunne's grasp and thudding into the net. Real 'Boy's Own' stuff!

As before, back came the home team launching raid after raid on Kelly's goal, but amongst this domination, another powerful Ham shot could have made it 2-0 but for a brilliant one handed save by Dunne. It was a cracking game and a great advert for Division Three.

Just as it appeared Argyle's challenge was fading, they finally equalised on 66 minutes. A corner was fired in and centre half Fred Molyneux met it with his head racing in towards goal. Kelly's first move was to pick the ball out of the net. Energised by this, Argyle were suddenly swarming all over North End scenting blood. As it happened, field marshal Hawkins and his men were in no mood to drive home empty handed, and with Plymouth generally in the ascendancy, the game drew to a close.

A good point to bring back home; and Ball could not have asked for any more effort from his men. Bobby Ham was pleased with himself too. *"When I saw the ball go in I was the happiest man on the field,"* he said after the game. On the face of it, it looked like North End may have picked up the bargain of the year. The busy attacker could not have made a better impression on his debut.

By midweek, the LEP was telling us that Ball had been offered and immediately agreed to sign a three year contract, back dated to his first day of North End employment. He had operated until now without any security. This move was made no doubt on the back of intense speculation that the Blackpool board of directors were discussing whether to offer Ball the manager's position at Bloomfield Road following the resignation of Les Shannon a couple of days before.

Shannon's decision to go had been made after a bizarre home fixture against Chelsea. Three nil up at half time, Shannon must have thought the 'Seasiders' had turned a corner in their quest for Division One survival. Just 45 minutes later, the home team trudged off 3-4 losers, slated by an angry home crowd. That afternoon was just about it for Shannon, who left immediately.

Ball, interviewed as he watched a practice match between North End and Blackpool at the Willow Farm training facility commented, *"I am delighted to accept the offer. I have become proud to be associated with Preston and am determined to lead them back to the top. The setup at Deepdale is much better than at Bloomfield Road, and we have big plans for the future."*

If a comment was ever made by a North End manager, intentional or not, that would endear him to the fans for ever, it was surely the above!

The players too, were benefiting under the Ball regime. Under his bonus scheme, they were collecting £20 (equivalent to £276 in 2015) per point if they are in the top four, jumping up to £25 (£345) per point in the top two places. With one game left in October their efforts had been rewarded to the tune of an extra £120 (£1658) on top of their wages. Very handy! But still much lower than today's farcical overpayments to players...

There is another thing that happened during that week that I wish to relate. I saw the most memorable goal I can ever recall from my childhood on television on Wednesday, October 28th.

The programme, 'Sportsnight with Coleman,' was just that. A mixture of all things sport fronted by the premier commentator of the time, David Coleman. This particular edition was largely devoted to a League Cup tie at Old Trafford between Manchester United and Chelsea. It was a mind blowing individual goal by George Best that has rented a far corner of my mind for evermore.

From around the half way line running at pace, shrugging off tackles and dangerous challenges, to rounding the keeper and slotting the ball home – it was wonderful. They still wheel out the clip whenever there is a feature about him on television, and still it seems just as fantastic. The school playground was buzzing the following morning before assembly with everybody asking, “Did you see Best last night?” Even my Dad, not really a fan of Best, conceded that it was as close to seeing Tom Finney again as you will get. It must have been a good goal then!

The final game of the month saw the return to Deepdale of a much appreciated former captain – Nobby Lawton. Lawton led North End to the FA Cup Final in 1964, after arriving from Manchester United. I only saw Lawton play a few times ‘live’ for North End due to my age, but I definitely recall the affection the fans held for him back in the mid 60’s.

He had since been transferred to Brighton & Hove Albion, who were seemingly going well. Although they had collected five points less than North End at this juncture, Ball was not underestimating them. *“Brighton are a very attractive team to watch, and it should be a great game.”*

As the team was announced, the name McNab wasn’t mentioned - again - apparently he was struggling to recover from a severely pulled muscle meaning that this would be yet another miss for our very trusty left back. Also out was Clive Clark with a bout of gastro enteritis - bad news after his recent exploits - he being replaced by Frank Lee on the left flank.

Despite not having won a game since the Mansfield clash, the dash down ‘Skeffy’ Road to the ground indicated that a good attendance would be present; indeed, it was officially recorded at 12,567.

It was to be a match of frustration. Yet another occasion where North End’s play deserved better than the 1-1 draw it achieved. The fans were disappointed – they had witnessed North End see teams off with their attacking style, and couldn’t fathom why it wasn’t being accompanied by a steady stream of wins...

Teams were arriving at Deepdale and their stated aim wasn’t to win – it was to frustrate and smother and get the big home crowd on North

End's back. However, if you could nick a goal against Preston, all the better – their crowd would lay into them even more....

That's just what happened in this game. Brighton initially sat back, inviting North End on. A combination of tough tackling and hoof-ball to break up any promising North End play was serving the visitors well as the game reached the half hour, then for North End disaster struck.

Brighton moved down the left in a rare sortie in to North End territory. After receiving the ball on the run from winger Peter O'Sullivan, inside left Dave Turner's shot made it across the North End goal line with the help of a deflection it seemed from Hawkins.

Despite increased efforts to break down the Brighton defensive ring, North End ended the half one down, to a chorus of shouts and boos.

I actually thought that was unfair because, "only one team wanted to play football", as the pundits often say these days.

The obligatory half time 'dishwatter' tasted even *worse* than usual.

Whatever Ball had said to North End during the interval seemed to have lifted them. Ham placed a shot just over the bar after being put through by Spavin, Wilson put Ingram through with a great ball but the centre forward couldn't profit, a Lee shot went over the bar, Ham then laid the ball off to Lee whose shot was saved, and enterprising play from Wilson forced two corners in quick succession - Brighton eventually clearing their lines. Brighton were under severe examination and finally cracked in the 70th minute. It was a simple Ham tap-in following the Brighton keeper's failure to hold onto an Ingram shot that leveled the scores and set up a frantic finish.

Spavin soon presented Ham with another great opportunity, the new signing losing control of the ball as he attempted to round the keeper. A superb Heppolette header put in Lee, but his shot screamed wide. The Gentry were in full cry now as George Ross popped up on the edge of the box only to see his shot go over the bar, and a Wilson corner was met perfectly by Heppolette; the header shaving the crossbar and top of the net with the keeper stranded.

A typical Brighton 'no nonsense' clearance, this time preventing any progress by North End's Bobby Ham

The whistle for full time blew, but there was no jeering this time. For all their inability to find the net for the winner, nobody who witnessed that game could say there was a lack of effort from North End...well, except probably their manager...

Of course, if you are hoping for promotion, home draws against mid table teams are not desirable. Ball had to solve this problem, and it seemed that in his post match press conference he was maybe pointing the finger at the inability of the wingers to supply the goal scoring machine called Ingram. *"We are working on this problem and will find a solution soon,"* he said. It was then that he uttered a remarkable quote, as if to infer that effort was lacking in some quarters.

"I would willingly break an arm one week for two points, and a leg for another win the next. What are one or two fractured limbs when we might be able to get out of the Third Division. The arms and legs will heal, but the points are lost forever. I expect all my players to be willing

to do the same – and I have no time for those who aren't."

A few words for the players to ponder as we said farewell to October.

George Ross - whether defending or overlapping at pace to create an attack - was indispensable. The full back pairing of Ross and McNab was easily the best in Division Three.

November

Doncaster Rovers, Barnsley, Swaps?, Rochdale, Transfer Bid, FA Cup Exit, Letters to the Editor, Chesterfield

A Friday evening fixture at Doncaster Rovers was North End's first away day in the new month. Ball had injury problems throughout the week following the Brighton game, the main area of concern being Ricky Heppolette, who received a shin injury during the 1-1 draw. It had failed to improve enough over the week, and he was left out of the squad. Jim McNab would still be on the sidelines too, so Ball named a squad of 14 for the South Yorkshire outing, keeping his options open until the last minute. The squad read:

Kelly, Ross, McMahon, Spark, Hawkins, Spavin, Wilson, Ham, Ingram, Lyall, Lee, Hughes, Irvine and Lloyd.

Doncaster Rovers were languishing at the bottom end of the table, but an upturn in form had seen them beat Barnsley away the previous weekend in the South Yorkshire derby. Managed by Lawrie McMenemy, who would lead Southampton to FA Cup glory at Wembley by the middle of the decade, Rovers could prove a difficult fixture for a North End team fully expected to win on League position alone.

And so it proved. North End had not shown any killer instinct by the 37th minute when Rovers took the lead. A Colin Clish free kick into the North End box was superbly headed home by centre half John Bird. Now, there's a name to remember!

In fact, despite a little more focused attacking in the second half the game was drifting away from North End, until Spavin crossed a ball into the box from the left wing. There was not a team mate in the box apart from an off balance David Hughes who appeared to be falling to the floor. Rovers defender Stuart Robertson, possibly thinking there was North End activity behind him, leapt high, twisted and headed the cross straight past his own keeper and under - not over - the bar, much to the delight of The Gentry in the 5,300 crowd who had faithfully trekked across the Pennines.

The 'gift' of a possible point was preciously treasured and North End saw out the rest of the game looking after it. It was, after all, another in the bag, and another away fixture ticked off.

Ball, as usual, didn't deliver the expected post match quotes such a laboured display probably deserved, seeming to reproach himself more than the players. *"If I could settle for a point in every away fixture, I would do so. We did not play well at times but we got the required result. We might have done better had we played 4-2-4 from the start, but I adopted a 4-3-3 formation in the first half which was wrong."*

Hot on the heels of the Doncaster Rovers fixture was a home game the following Monday evening against Barnsley. News from the North End camp was that Clive Clark was now fit, and the indications were that Ball wanted the speedy and widely decorated winger to become his first choice on the left flank. He was now being attached to the squad whenever available, unlike earlier in the season.

Walking to the ground, once again the indications were of a decent sized crowd. In fact, just over 11,000 turned out for what was to be a superb display by the home side.

Barnsley, in keeping with the previous visitors to Deepdale adopted an immediate defensive and brutal approach to the game. There was something different about North End though, it was obvious they had been working at nullifying such strategies and it was an investment that would bring due reward.

From the 17th minute when Ham poked in a mishandled McMahon cross by the Barnsley keeper, North End never looked back. Enterprising play from the midfield, with Spavin and Lyall superbly routing play through the 'reborn' Clark caused the visitors countless problems. Despite the Barnsley players dishing out the bad tackles, the referee remained very lenient, booking only Barrie Murphy in the first half.

North End stuck to their task well, and were rewarded with a second goal just before the half time whistle. Spavin floated a free kick to the inside right position were Ingram moved forward and beat the keeper with a well placed header.

After the mugs of tea it was more of the same all round. While Barnsley tried to kick chunks out of North End, North End completely outclassed them. However, the visitors pegged one back mid way through the half when Dearden shot past Kelly at the second attempt after the Irishman had blocked his first try.

Despite continued punishment and incredibly only the name of Barnsley midfielder Norman Dean adding any further ink to the referee's notebook, North End remained aloof and got their just reward around five minutes before the end - Lyall clinching the game with a 25 yard thunderbolt that sent the fans home in a happy frame of mind.

Ball was in a happy mood too, post match. *"This time the game spoke for itself. I'll leave it to you,"* he joked to the journalists present. *"We played like a First Division team in the first half and only Barnsley's tough tactics kept the score down."*

Clark and Lyall were superb on the night, but in truth all the team played well.

By Wednesday, Blackpool were casting their shadow over Deepdale again. Marooned with Burnley at the foot of Division One, and with Jimmy Meadows in temporary charge following Les Shannon's resignation, they were looking for new talent to shore up their ailing season. Casting their eyes no further than 15 miles inland for the third time this season was surely a massive compliment to North End. Blackpool just couldn't keep away.

First target was Heppolette. Second target was Ball. This time it was North End's Heppolette and Lloyd in a swap for Blackpool's Fred Pickering and reserve forward Ronnie Brown. Oh, and they would throw in £25,000 too. Pickering was actually Blackpool's current first team centre forward; so what was going on here?! True, he had hit a hat trick on his last visit to Deepdale to send us down- but to offer him like this suggested something was awry.

Apparently the proposal was discussed at board level, Ball adding, *"There have been no official bids made to me. We are doing very well here and in a good position in the table. Everybody is happy here and we think we are going places."* That was pleasing to hear. It sounded like Ball's input, should he be asked for it by the Board would be, "No thanks!"

Nothing further was ever mentioned about the proposed swap and thankfully it all faded away. Phew!

Friday's fitness roll call at Deepdale prior to the home game against Rochdale showed that Ricky Heppolette's injury was mending but he was only fit enough to be considered as substitute. Jim McNab remained a long term casualty. The team was:

Kelly, Ross, McMahon, Spark, Hawkins, Spavin, Wilson, Ham, Ingram, Lyall, Clark, sub Heppolete.

North End sat fifth in the table with 22 points from 18 games, still five points behind leaders Fulham. Over the last 11 games, North End were the form team, taking 15 points from a possible 22, winning five and drawing five, with just one defeat. Statistics such as those demonstrated the consistent performances Ball was now extracting from his players, and that the platform for a possible promotion push was being well and truly cemented into place.

It was a crisp and cold autumn afternoon as North End kicked off towards the Kop. Rochdale, languishing in the bottom four of the section, were given plenty to think about as their hosts launched offensive after offensive. The wingers, Wilson and Clark were drilling their way forward down the flanks once again supplying the ammunition for Ham and Ingram to fire at the Rochdale goal. In fact, North End's opener after a catalogue of near misses was entirely down the wide men – as it was Wilson who rose splendidly to head home a corner from Clark around the 20th minute.

However, for David Tennant, the Rochdale keeper there was no respite. Indeed, had he been blessed with his actor namesake's powers, it would have been wise to jump into the Tardis and reappear at a more favourable venue. Unfortunately though this wasn't Dr Who stood between the goal posts in front of the Kop!

After another flurry of activity in the 'Dale box, North End were denied a second when Tennant fumbled a well placed Wilson cross, the ball seemingly hitting the hand of a defender on the way down. As the ball ran free, Ham seized his chance and prodded it over the line via the post....or so we all thought. With the ball seemingly hacked back into play from a good foot over the 'Dale goal line, the referee amazingly waved 'play - on,' much to the home crowd's disapproval.

The home fans didn't have to wait long though. Just before half time, Ingram shot into a ruck of players in front of the goal, the ball conveniently rolling out into the path of Ham, who rifled it home ....well, at least as far over the line as his previous attempt....

Half time arrived and the 'Dale players trooped off looking exhausted. A great display of attacking football by North End that merited several more goals than the two actually registered, was acknowledged with heavy applause.

It took just four minutes of the second half to knock North End's game completely out of kilter. Hawkins conceded a free kick just outside the penalty area, and up stepped Norman Whitehead – 'Dales liveliest forward - to breach the North End defensive wall; his shot nestling in the back of the net via the post.

This seemed to cause the onset of a strange case of 'the jitters' in the North End team. They were suddenly transformed from Brazil into Barrow; from the sure minded into ditherers. That was the bad news....the good news was that 'Dale were so poor they couldn't capitalise on this self inflicted North End torment.

This lasted for about 15 minutes, when the home side recovered sufficiently to at least dominate proceedings, even if not with the complete control of the first half.

Ham had a shot blocked by the keeper and Ingram looked to have been upended in the 'Dale area to all and sundry; except that is the referee, who waved 'play-on.' Wilson cut in at pace from the wing and crashed a shot just over the bar, and another Ingram chance came to nothing as the keeper dropped thankfully onto the loose ball.

Meanwhile....Whitehead was seeing opportunities on the break materialise, his best effort of securing the equaliser occurring when he beat two men with a burst of speed when put through with a clear path on North End's goal near the centre circle. A stubbed toe and the ball gently rolling towards Kelly put paid to that scare; the home crowd cheering loudly.

A couple of minutes later, the same move this time utilising David Cross, (who would later lead many a First Division forward line), resulted in Hawkins incurring the referee's wrath by delivering a tackle that would have felled a mature oak tree as Cross pulled the trigger just outside the box.

With around seven minutes left, Wilson was injured to the point of no return and was replaced by substitute Heppolette. As injury time approached, a superb move by the home team finally sealed the game in some style.

George Ross hurtled down the right wing for the umpteenth time, and

crossed superbly. Ingram, the target, moved across the face of goal to meet the ball, and glance it down and towards Lyall who was hovering around the penalty spot. Noted for his powerful shooting, Lyall met the ball on the volley, and a millisecond later it was duly collected by the net, with Tenant still airborne waving his arms.

The score line now looked a more accurate reflection of the game, and the largest Deepdale league crowd of the season to date of over 13,000 went home satisfied. The win lifted North End into third place, behind Bristol Rovers and, leaders on goal average, Fulham. After 19 games 24 points had been collected, three behind the two teams above.

Final thought on this particular weekend must go to Ball. Back in September he had pointed out after a tepid display at Villa Park against a then all-conquering home team, that the scribes questioning North End's credentials would be better employed seeing how Villa went on at places like Halifax later in the season. That match up was happening as North End played Rochdale. Villa lost 2-1 and North End moved above them in the table...

Monday's edition of the LEP brought news of possible further dabbling in the transfer market by North End. Following glowing reports fed back by Peter Doherty, Ball had made a bid of £20,000 for Wrexham's Arfon Griffiths, a diminutive midfielder, but by all accounts a keen tackler and creative too. Immediately my cynical mind put two and two together and convinced itself that Ricky Heppolette was probably going to be sold on.

The report also revealed that North End were monitoring Bolton's winger Gordon Taylor, but the club's valuations were poles apart.

In the event, this was just another transfer story that fizzled out, but a good insight into quality of player Ball was looking at.

It was FA Cup week too. FA Cup first round, that is, as North End's new status in the lower echelons of the Football League now demanded. The numbered balls had been pulled out of the velvet bag at Lancaster Gate a couple of weeks before. "Preston North End...will play...Chester."

Surely this was a hurdle we could overcome?

With a couple of days to go, injury news surfaced from the bowels of Deepdale. Dave Wilson still had a badly bruised shin that had forced him to limp off against Rochdale the previous weekend and leading scorer Gerry Ingram, just like John and Yoko the year before, had been in bed all week... but only with 'flu. However, both were hoping to be fit to start the FA Cup tie.

By Friday evening, the promising news was that both had been named in the squad along with long term absentee, Jim McNab. The news that he was back in full training was a real boost – and not just in terms of the imminent Cup clash. In the event, Mc Nab was given a final run out in the reserves to give him some vital match practice.

The dreary November weather that greeted the teams as they ran out was a big clue. It was a very poor game, unfortunately played out in front of a quite massive first round gate of over 15,000.

North End simply never got going, or more accurately were never allowed to get going. Maybe it was hard for North End to get very interested in this game, with all their recent progress in the League. Chester's workmanlike display and refusal to be intimidated by a much bigger stage than they were used to, deserves credit.

It was North End that took the lead though around ten minutes before half time. After displaying absolutely no rhythm or panache in their play to that point, a Ross centre was headed home by Heppolette with some style. For the remaining ten minutes, the North End we knew and loved returned, and it was Heppolette again popping up in the area, who was within an ace of putting North End two up, pushing the ball just wide.

The second half soon developed into a re-run of the majority of the first.

It was Chester who were the more methodical in their approach, North End looking as if they may have taken this tie as a 'given.' No real surprise then, when on 70 minutes the ever lively Alan Tarbuck who latched on to the ball in the North End box and drove it firmly under the diving Kelly. (It must have impressed Ball, as Tarbuck would sign for Preston during the following season).

Sticking to their game plan – which quite simply meant hounding the North End midfield and stifling the wingers – nearly paid out the ultimate reward for the visitors, with Keith Webber shooting just wide in the last minute with Kelly well beaten.

Ball, ever protective of his team, remained upbeat at the post match press conference. *"We never looked like losing, and had only ourselves to blame for missing chances. They equalised because of our slackness, but even after that I knew we would not be beaten."*

Another couple of injuries had to be assessed before the Wednesday replay at Chester. Full backs McMahon and Ross were the walking wounded and Ball added the now fully fit McNab, along with reserve full backs John Ritchie and Bert Patrick to the coach party.

It was good to have Jim McNab back and available again. Having served Sunderland very well for a long time, he did just as good a job for us in his later career. With his droopy moustache, he was a dead ringer for Jason King, the star detective of one of the better TV series of the late 60's, *Department S*. Well...from a distance anyway!

Whatever North End's problem was on Saturday, it continued for the full 90 minutes of the replay at Sealand Road. A more inglorious Cup exit you could not wish to have.

Ball played both McNab and Patrick as direct replacements for Ross and McMahon, kept Lyall as substitute and dropped Wilson altogether for Hughes. In the event, Patrick never displayed any form of the kind Ross had been producing, Hughes for Wilson didn't seem to work and Lyall's eventual emergence from the touchline was the only time the midfield seem to function. As team performances go it was completely haywire.

After Chester mysteriously dominated North End once more - Eddie Loyden drilling home the winner after a Kelly block - Ball felt the need to pen a special piece in the LEP about the two Chester games to try and explain exactly what happened.

He pulled no punches. In an extraordinary article, he basically posed the same question to the fans several different ways. It always came back to, *"Do you want me to sacrifice our realistic promotion ambitions for maybe one or two glamour cup ties at best followed by an inevitable exit, then realising we had blown our REAL big chance."*

Other telling comments included,

"...the players knew before they went out that I would not be breathing fire and brimstone if we lost,"

"...If anyone really thinks that a Third Division club is going to lift the FA Cup, they are deluded,"

"...I would like to remind fans that there are other objectives even more important than a few hours excitement of cup tie football."

His closing paragraph, *"I believe in the logic of what I have said and I'm sure the defeat in the FA Cup need not be viewed with too much dismay by a club fighting for promotion. It's a disappointment, yes, but it doesn't have to be a disaster,"* nailed his view down firmly, and as far as he was concerned, closed the book on the subject.

With a promotion platform in place after three months hard work, Ball was not willing to risk seeing anything stand in North End's way. Personally speaking, I didn't really want to argue with Ball's view, especially in this particular season. But some could. North End had been success starved for far too long.

North End had a proud history in the FA Cup, an annual event looked forward too by fans both young and old. The *Football Post* mail bag was full to bursting with the fans views on Ball's open letter.

The star, 'Two Guinea Letter' composed by Mr. JG of Broadgate, was typical...

"Once again North End have added another degrading chapter to those already written over the last few seasons... Is it not more feasible, Mr. Ball, that a good Cup run will improve player confidence, attract bigger crowds and as a consequence bring in more revenue?...Ball's dream of Second Division football next season with his present attitude and ideas is as far away as the moon."

Fans vote with their feet, so it would be interesting to see how many would decide to stay away when North End next turned out at Deepdale.

However it was Saltergate, Chesterfield that was North End's next stop. 'The Spireites' were one of those tricky teams to play against. Hovering around tenth in the table, they neither scored or conceded many goals; were tall at the back and were far from a pushover in this division.

A good performance was necessary for Ball to banish the lingering memories of the FA Cup disappointment with Chester.

Ball fielded: *Kelly,Ross, McNab, Spark, Hawkins, Spavin, Lyall, Ham, Ingram, Heppolette, Clark, Sub Wilson.*

Thankfully, North End returned to something like the form they had been showing before the Chester 'experience'. With Ball's prediction that the team would perform much better than in the FA Cup, it was a certain trepidation that The Gentry made their way to Chesterfield, some undoubtedly thinking, "had the bubble burst?"

Although they only came home with a point from a goalless draw, it was another away point, a clean sheet and an extension of the unbeaten

League run to seven games. Agreed, they dropped to fourth in the table but they were still only three points behind top spot.

Ball certainly set out his team to win. Playing 4-3-3, with Lyall playing alongside Spavin and Heppolette in midfield, North End launched a string of attacks as they completely dominated the centre of the park. Indeed Lyall, was the best player on view. He had certainly hit a purple patch, and his speed and ability to fire crossfield balls accurately to feet was a joy to watch. His feeding of Clark down the right, (another player bang in form), was quite brilliant and the winger was causing his marker much frustration and distress as he regularly danced around him at some lick. Indeed the defender was booked after scything down Clark once too often for the referee's liking.

Chesterfield did their share of attacking too, but neither team could complete a move by finding the net.

Late in the second half Clark cut inside beautifully at pace after being set up superbly by a Lyall through ball. He fired a 25 yard screamer that didn't dip quite enough to find its way under the crossbar with the goalkeeper well beaten.

The problem on this particular day was that the miserly Chesterfield defence had Ingram and Ham in such a vice like hold they didn't really find any goal scoring opportunities on offer.

After another clash that laid Clark out, he made his way to the dugouts and asked Ball if he could be substituted after a head collision, only for the manager to get to his feet and push the winger back onto the pitch, telling him in the process that he was playing far too well for that!

As was becoming a regular feature of North End away games, Ball decided about 15 minutes from time that the point they held was to be secured. This was fine in theory, but in practice invited teams on somewhat, and this game was no exception. Chesterfield threw everything forward sensing a late winner was on the cards, but Kelly (with three fine saves), Hawkins, Spark, McNab and in particular Ross, stood firm under the onslaught.

Ball's claim afterwards that the team did *"All I asked,"* was correct. They attacked for nigh on 70 minutes before taking another precious away point back to Deepdale. It was a good day's work.

Clive Clark – too much class and far too quick for the Chesterfield defence

December

Gillingham, Torquay United, Granada TV Coverage, Tranmere Rovers

As Saturday, December 5th and the home game with bottom of the table Gillingham edged closer, Ball was in a cautious mood.

Far from urging people to mark their Littlewoods coupon 'banker home win' he was dreading the prospect of playing the men from Kent.

"The clubs at the bottom are all difficult to beat. They have nothing to lose, and everyone plays at the back whacking and kicking. I watched Gillingham at Rochdale recently and they had a ten man defence. They had three shots on goal, scored on the breakaway and won 1-0. Beating a team like this has been a problem for Preston in the past – you get frustrated, lose your composure and maybe get your full backs forward once too often, then bang you are in trouble."

Despite his misgivings, he named an unchanged squad from the previous outing at Chesterfield.

As kick off neared, it just about registered audibly over the ex-Colditz tannoy system that Heppolette was the substitute, with Wilson back on the right wing. When they kicked off it was apparent that North End were playing 4-2-4, obviously wanting to combat the Gillingham defence that we had been warned would be ten man strong.

It took just seven minutes to break the deadlock. Clark, continuing his run of fine form, hurtled down the left wing and fired in a low dangerous cross which was met and controlled by Ingram. He passed the ball sideways for Ham to hit a hard low shot past the sprawling keeper.

The pattern continued throughout the game. Control of midfield by Lyall and Spavin; ball fed to Clark or Wilson. Speed down the flank, then a cross for Ingram and Ham. This adopted style was responsible for countless efforts on goal and North End should have had a cricket score by the end. Ham hit the post and crossbar with snap shots in the penalty area and Ingram also hit the crossbar with a header.

At times Gillingham's desperate and, (as Ball predicted), packed defence kicked anywhere for safety as North End overwhelmed them. But somehow their goal remained intact. So did North End's - but for wholly different reasons. Gillingham's preoccupation with survival meant that North End's defence was camped around the half way line feeding the ball to the midfielders, should it come their way.

Clark, Ham and Spavin were the stand out players for North End, witnessed by a crowd of just over 10,000, down by 3,000 compared to the last home league game, and 5,000 for that fateful Chester FA Cup tie. It certainly looked like there was an arguable case that the terrace critics of Ball's attitude regarding that game were protesting by staying away....

He would have plenty of time to reflect on those comments of a fortnight ago, as North End now had a blank weekend - it was the second round of the FA Cup.

An away friendly was hastily arranged at Grimsby Town to keep those North End limbs loose, with the Lilywhites coming away with a 3-2 win.

Grimsby started quickly and were two goals to the good before Clark, still enjoying a rich seam of form, placed a header past the keeper to reduce the deficit. He hadn't finished there; shortly afterwards he embarked on a typical run, brilliantly beating three men in the process before slotting the ball home. Grimsby retaliated and shaved the post with a snap shot before the mugs of tea and oranges were served.

North End 'clinched' the game in the second half when a Grimsby defender pushed the ball over his own line when not really under serious pressure.

Not serious Saturday football, but a good workout. North End looked a good side – definitely a couple of cuts above Grimsby.

The secondary school that I attended drew upon the primary schools in the Deepdale and Moor Park area amongst others and by midweek there was a definite buzz in the playground air.

The rumour had started that North End's game with Torquay United had been chosen by Granada TV for their Sunday afternoon highlights programme 'Football.' The lads who lived near to the ground had seen a Granada van in the vicinity of North End, and by Friday it was reported that a huge crane was sat in the main car park behind the West Stand.

"So what?" the young fan of today would say. Well, back in those days there were just two or three hour long football programmes on television *per week* – nothing like today's wall to wall saturation coverage. It was a big novelty then to see your home team on television; but then again not generally a good experience for North End fans, or the team for that matter, who usually saved their worst performances for the cameras.

December 19th 1970 was typically one of those grey, cloudy and chilly days reserved for the north west of England late in the year. Wrapped up well, as I neared the ground the 'crane cameraman' in his lofty position came into view. So at least that confirmed we were to be on the telly; the prayer I offered up next was for it to be a great North End performance…

North End kicked off towards the Kop, but before any latecomers had found a spot, they were one down. Make that two down after around 20 minutes. Total disaster!

It was Kelly, Eire international and keeper of great quality who literally and inexplicably 'set the ball rolling.' A harmless looking punt forward from Mick Cave, the Torquay winger, slipped through his arms and proceeded to bounce over the goal line almost in slow motion.

I recall thinking how harsh it was that he received ironic cheers from some home fans every time he caught the ball from then on. After all the occasions he had kept North End alive in games over the years, he deserved sympathy, not jeers.

North End finally got to work. However, a prolonged spell of all out attack ended in unbelievable fashion when a rare Torquay raid in the North End box saw John Rudge glance home a header from a centre by Cliff Jackson. More stunned silence, then angry shouts from the home crowd. This was turning into a nightmare - and one the whole of the Granada (NW England) region would share on Sunday afternoon...

North End started again. By now, Ball not a man for containing his feelings, was occasionally stood outside of the dugout urging the team forward. North End were grabbing this 'lost' game by the scruff of the neck and dragging it back into play. Attack after attack was launched by the outstanding midfield pair of Lyall and Spavin. A Ham pile driver went a fraction wide as did a Clark chip. Ingram headed just over - twice; and then had a 15 yard shot on the turn saved. It was exciting stuff. Suddenly the fans attitude had changed from 'doom and gloom' to a much more positive, 'we need three to win' attitude.

Andy Donnelly, the Torquay keeper was having the game of his life. A string of acrobatic and spectacular saves were keeping North End at bay until Ingram found himself without a marker around ten yards from goal. Showing good control of a difficult cross he managed to side foot the ball home firmly past the sprawling Donnelly to finally reduce the arrears. The goal was just desserts for North End, and the half time discussion had everyone agreeing that a comeback was definitely 'on.'

After the ten minute rest, North End again went on the attack. Lyall was even more prominent and was becoming involved further up the field, supporting Ham and Ingram. It didn't take long for North End to finally achieve parity, and to set up a thrilling finale.

A ball from the left was played into the Torquay box and eventually found Lyall who drilled home a scorching shot from 15 yards into the right of Donnelly's net. This sent the crowd into euphoria. What a goal - and on television too!

Could North End achieve the impossible? This game was proving yet again that Ball's motivational skills were second to none, as a comeback of such proportions was never an option in recent seasons.

With the crowd still buzzing from the after effects of Lyall's net buster, he stunned the crowd by almost replicating it once more. In a similar move - this time teed up by Ingram - Lyall let fly from almost the same spot as before. Donnelly dived as before. Donnelly missed it as before. However the goal post was in the way... unlike before. After the ball thudded into the base of the post, it cannoned away harmlessly, much to the visitors' relief.

All this action seemed to shake Torquay into a rally, and for the rest of the match the players from both teams put in a massive effort. North End did receive a body blow however in that Bobby Ham had to leave the field gingerly, in what was later described as 'possible ligament strain.'

The match ended in a 2-2 draw. Even though it wasn't a win, it was without doubt the most exciting game of the season to date at Deepdale, taped too by Granada for posterity...or so I thought...

I hung around the centre line on the West Paddock side after the game, as I wanted to see exactly what happened post match in regard to the television presentation. There were around 30 other kids and a few adults present too, and with the stewards just telling us to behave and be quiet, it was all very illuminating.

George Lyall's blistering shot beats everybody to put North End back on level terms with Torquay United

Lyall's second pile driver crashes into the base of the Torquay post, denying North End the lead in the TV game

First, Gerald Sinsdadt did a piece to camera that was obviously an early evening trailer for the Sunday broadcast. It was hard to hear exactly what was said, but I heard him say the words, "excitement" and "thrillling." Sadly, I cannot remember if Alan Ball Snr was hooked out of the dressing room for a few words, as by the time I glanced down at my watch, half an hour had passed and I had to hastily make my way home.

So, what better than contacting ITV some 45 years later to see if I could purchase a copy of the game from their well publicised archives? It would be just fantastic to see it all again, warts and all. I fired off the email quite excited at the prospect. Sod the expense!

I needn't have bothered.

The two inch video tape of the game that was 'thrilling' and full of 'excitement,' *"has probably been wiped,"* I was told. The librarian had checked every which way, but the message coming back was always, 'No Copy.'

"They had the less than bright idea back then that nobody would want to see old television again, so saved money by wiping archived tapes and re-using them," the librarian explained, adding *"they would be sacked if that happened today."* Many actually survived - I have quite a few in my collection, but the thought of that 'North End Classic' possibly morphing into a 1971 episode of *'Stars on Sunday'* with Jess Yates on the organ fills me with distress, despair and the shivers - not in any particular order I might add - but awful all the same. What a waste!

On Monday, the LEP was giving a clearer insight into what happened during Saturday's game. It had emerged that a downhearted Kelly after his howler in the first half, had been immediately singled out by Ball during the half time break. It was a very positive message that Ball delivered to his keeper in front of his team mates however....

"You are in my team next week and are in the side for the rest of the season. You are a great goalkeeper."

This must have been a huge lift for Kelly, who was a cornerstone of the team and in later years, the club. After making his worst ever mistake - in front of the TV cameras too - hearing that reassurance *must* have lifted his spirits. It was confirmed that Bobby Ham had received knee ligament damage but no firm news as to how long this key striker would be absent for.

As the Christmas holidays started for us poor deprived schoolchildren, North End had just one more fixture to fulfil in 1970. An away day in Birkenhead, visiting Tranmere Rovers was the Boxing Day treat, North End hoping to take their unbeaten run in the League into double figures.

With Ham being absent, Irvine returned to the squad hoping for a prolonged run in the first team. Ball had yet to decide on his final formation, but named the following to travel through the Mersey Tunnel:

Kelly, Ross, McNab, Spark, Hawkins, Spavin, Wilson, Irvine, Ingram, Lyall, Clark and Heppolette.

As it turned out, Ball had his mind made up for him regarding the final team selection, as Ingram pulled out at the last moment with a chest infection. Thus he went with a powerful looking 4-3-3 formation, with Lyall, Spavin and Heppolette spread across the middle.

North End went behind early however, following a ten minute spell of all out attack. Inevitable gaps at the back appeared and lower division super striker Ken Beamish hardly needed a second invitation to put Rovers one up. North End rallied immediately and it was an Alex Spark foray into the Tranmere half that set it all up. Pushing forward with some purpose he centred the ball into the box where Clark converted the chance to notch his first League goal of the season.

North End continued to dominate their hosts up to half time with near misses from Ingram and Heppolette foiling their progress.

The second half began at a decent pace. There was further defensive hesitation, this time by Kelly. Trying to deal with a Beamish centre from the right, the umming and ahhing enabled Malcolm Moore to eventually prod the ball home.

At this stage it was all very frustrating. Two self inflicted gift goals for Rovers saw them lead after North End had looked a classier attacking outfit from the start.

The North End attacks continued. It was Heppolette who finally fired the Lilywhites to parity, his volley screaming into the net following some neat approach work and centre from Spavin.

Then we had an incredible few minutes as former North Ender Paul Crossley first handed North End a 2-3 lead and within a few minutes took it off them again - in some style.

Crossley just couldn't physically avoid a crisply served Clark centre and the resulting deflection wrong footed Frank Lane, the Tranmere keeper and bounced into the home net. He trudged back towards the centre line, but his misery wouldn't last long.

Collecting a clearance on the edge of the North End box while at full pelt, he let fly an unstoppable shot that left Kelly pawing at thin air. The home fans loved it; back to 3-3 and all to play for. Indeed, there was still time for a brace of Lyall 'trademark' pile drivers to be deflected away by Lane and a Heppolette header to fly the wrong side of the Tranmere crossbar.

It was without doubt excellent festive fare. Yet another away point gathered, but the worry was that North End were gifting goals to the opposition, and coming away with only a point when they had done more than enough attacking to fairly claim the other. Perhaps a New Year's resolution to be more ruthless was needed.

It was reported that Blackpool – their officials permanently sat in the North End stands it seemed - had been monitoring Lyall over the past four games. Meanwhile, North End had made a bid of £12,500 for an "unnamed youngster" with a Fourth Division club. Talks were apparently ongoing.

This was indeed the start of Ball's protracted, but eventually doomed bid to secure Kevin Keegan from Scunthorpe United. You have to admit it; he certainly had an eye for football talent.

So as the year drew to a close, North End stood fourth in the Division, still just two points behind Fulham and Villa but four behind leaders Bristol Rovers.

A talking point during the season was North End's 'Falling Wall' free kick routine. The four North End players would disperse in all directions as Spavin ran forward to take the kick - obscuring, confusing and distracting the opposition defenders.

January

Nonsense, Shrewsbury Town, Swansea City, Boo Boys, Transfer Speculation, Walsall, Chesterfield

Watching from the sidelines was the order of the day for North End on the first Saturday of the New Year. Rotherham United, penciled in as their opponents at Deepdale for the 2nd of January were still in the FA Cup and drawn to play Leeds United at Millmoor. However the nation was under very wintry conditions and this tie, amongst others, would fall foul of the weather.

There was no friendly lined up this time for the North End's 'weekend off' - but there was no time for putting their feet up. Instead the LEP sports page displayed a photograph of Ball watching his squad stamina building by repeatedly run up and down the considerable grass banking at the Preston Harriers athletics track on London Road.

I will digress from North End for a few paragraphs, as one FA Cup tie that was played was in the North West - at Blackpool, with their brand new manager Bob Stokoe watching his team beat West Ham United 4-0. It *seemed* quite a triumph - until the full facts came out a day or two later...

The way things were going for our friends on the coast, to achieve that level of performance, Blackpool would have needed half of the West Ham team to be playing with hangovers. Incredibly it was soon revealed they were; courtesy of the Moore & Greaves Social Committee booking a *'Blackpool Night Out'* at ex-boxer Brian London's nightclub!

Assistant coach Jimmy Meadows, who had been acting manager until Stokoe's appointment, was known to, shall we say, be 'outspoken' at times. He couldn't resist the 'shooting from the hip' after the match telling the press that incredibly, *"Bobby Moore was overrated and the **worst defender in the world.**"*

As they say these days, those comments went 'viral.'

By Monday, Meadows was still the talking point rather than the 'momentous' victory. Hilariously, Stokoe was forced to issue a public rebuke to Meadows, reminding him basically who was in charge at Blackpool, and that he would do the talking about the football in future.

One of the best responses came from the LEP's Alan Hubbard. In a stinging piece, he encapsulated most football fans views in a nutshell. Mentioning the obvious unprofessionalism of Meadows criticising Moore in such derogatory terms, he added ironically, *"Apart from anything else it exposes Meadows as the **worst judge of a player in the world.**"*

It goes without saying that Moore was every kids hero in the 60's and early 70's - well those who followed football anyway. He was simply magnificent as a player and captain. Alright; he had been tempted to 'have a few' with his mates - and was guilty as charged - but despite this indiscretion, Jimmy Meadows' opinion was totally unnecessary. In fact, he was the one left with more tarnish on his reputation; Moore taking the medicine and never commenting on any aspect of the incident.

North End meanwhile received better news regarding Bobby Ham. Just a fortnight after having his leg put in plaster due to a medial ligament injury, the cast was due to be removed with Ham anxious to return to training. Ball was keen to see him return as soon as possible; whereas trainer Harry Hubbick was much more cautious....Ham may need a *further week* to recover! Was it really a ligament injury? If so, how different from today, when such damage is deemed to be quite serious.

Ball had sent Peter Doherty to the FA Cup tie at The Hawthorns to keep tabs on Keegan once again, and the reports coming back were good. North End's bid of £12,500 still lay on the table, with Scunthorpe only willing to deal at £25,000. News of Ball's pursuit of this obvious talent was all over the national newspapers by now and it only needed another club to move in with a bid nearer the mark for all his work to be wasted.

There was a temporary deal did go through however; Gerry Stewart, the reserve keeper was loaned out to Huddersfield Town. Indeed, with Huddersfield keeper Terry Poole having broken his leg in the FA Cup tie with Birmingham City, Stewart would maybe get the chance of some of that first team time he obviously craved.

Interestingly, it was reported too that Peter Dobing of Stoke City had been banned for six weeks (potentially anything up to ten games), because he had received - wait for it - three bookings within a calendar year! This was then unbelievably extended to nine weeks as his second booking had resulted in a three week 'suspended sentence' which was now gleefully tagged on by the Lancaster Gate hierarchy. How would today's superstars cope with such punishment?!

By Friday, the big team news was that Ham had 'recovered' and would play against Shrewsbury Town at Deepdale. Irvine would make way for Ingram, Ross (groin strain) for McMahon and, as usual, the last place would be taken by Wilson or Heppolette depending on the formation Ball finally decided to go with.

From what I can see in my scrapbook notes, it was a cold cloudy day with a decent crowd of just under 12,000 inside Deepdale for what was really a 'must win' game; North End drawing three of their previous four outings.

As it turned out, it was one of those strange affairs that North End seemed to be saddled with – do all the attacking, miss lots of chances, win the game but send some supporters home unhappy. I must say that never applied to me as far as I can recall. I had witnessed season after season of misery; it didn't really bother me too much how we won!

North End, as usual at Deepdale, came out all guns blazing. Kicking toward the Town End, Ball had decided to go with a 4-2-4 formation, meaning Wilson got the nod ahead of Heppolette this time. After only eight minutes, a penalty was awarded to North End. After good approach work down the flank and a pass inside from McNab to Ingram, the centre forward moved into the box only for Shrewsbury goalkeeper Bob Tooze to whip the forwards legs from under him as he was in the process of shooting.

The penalty was executed with accuracy, firmly and positively hit. From behind the Town End goal, the goalkeeper guessed wrong and dived east, while watching the ball - and his hopes of saving it - go west.

It's not a fabrication to say that the entire first half was spent in and around the proximity of the Shrewsbury penalty area; such was North End's domination. It was just that they couldn't score!

Ingram was the main culprit. On four separate occasions he fluffed golden scoring opportunities, while Ham, looking for his 100th League goal, did beat the keeper with a shot only to see it cleared off the line by Shrews' right back, Tony Gregory. By 30 minutes, Shrewsbury had not registered one shot at North End's goal but were clinging on, just the one goal behind.

Following the goal line clearance, Ham went very close again as Wilson, beating his marker and taking the ball further forward, crossed low and hard across the face of the Shrews' goal. Ham's dash and outstretched leg missed the ball by inches, with nobody manning the net.

The first the visitors saw of Alan Kelly was five minutes or so before the half ended, with centre forward Terry Harkin picking out the roofing sheets that adorned the Kop roof with a lame effort.

The second half did see some forward movement from the visitors, but it was North End who went 2-0 up. A teasing midfield through pass committed Tooze to advance well away from his line. He hadn't reckoned with speed of the charging Ingram and Ham and found himself caught as the ball bounced exquisitely upwards for Ingram to lob the ball on the run into the vacated net.

As the game drew to a close, a slow handclap started up from some fans. I wasn't sure why then, and I'm no wiser now as to why this happened. Surely it wasn't directed at North End....was it? They had besieged the Shrews' goal from the first minute until the last. Ok, they didn't win 25-0 but surely 2-0 would suffice – it was two points earned, and extended the unbeaten league run to eleven games.

Bobby Ham is inches away from converting Dave Wilson's hard low cross into a goal against Shrewsbury

"What do we have to do to please the crowd?" groaned Ball in the press conference. *"I'm always grateful for a win, two points are two points. The supporters should be happy."*

He went on to explain that after Ingram's second goal he got the message out to *'keep it tight'* and *'go for a professional win.'*

It should be noted that the players did exactly as Ball told them. It certainly *was* a 'professional win.'

Midweek brought the latest news on the Kevin Keegan transfer saga. He had been watched once more and, once more, the reports were glowing. There was a touch of frustration evident though when Ball was quoted as saying, "I would make a bid of £20,000 tomorrow, for he will be worth £90,000 in a couple of years - but we are short of money and we wouldn't have any left over for anybody else that we might need. The trouble now is there are seven other clubs interested too...."

It was so typical of North End. Ball had given every indication in his short tenure that he knew exactly what to look for in a player. He should have been backed on this issue instead of the old style dithering approach of the board, which we hoped had been a thing of the past. Heaven knows were North End would have got to in the mid 70's if those Directors had been brave.

Friday night's away fixture at The Vetch Field, Swansea was looming in the distance. Ball could call upon a fit George Ross once again, the ever reliable full back having recovered from his groin strain.

Thirteen would travel, with Ball probably reverting to his favoured away formation of 4-3-3. Since their draw back in October at Deepdale, slowly but surely the' Swans' had been creeping up the table. They now stood just above half way, but their improvement meant North End's task would be all that much harder.

North End left very early on Friday for the trip to South Wales; the players being promised a 'busman's holiday' reward of sorts by Ball - the party would drop in at the Walsall v Gillingham game on the way back through the Midlands on Saturday afternoon - the Lilywhites being due to play there the following week.

There was yet more news on Keegan - Ball had upped his bid by £5,000 which at least had triggered a Scunthorpe United board of directors meeting. We would have to be patient for a little longer.

In what the LEP described as the 'most blatant crime since the 'great train robbery' North End left the city of Swansea with just a point to add to their accumulated tally of 31, thanks entirely to the apparently absurd decision of referee, Mr. Maurice Washer of Bristol.

North End trooped off the pitch heads down, Washer having awarded a last minute penalty for the home team, duly converted, for a 'push' that left the North End defence looking at each other, scratching their heads.

With a clutch of First Division managers watching from the stands, North End had played all the football by the time they opened the scoring in the 35th minute. The Spavin, Lyall and Heppolette triumvirate had assumed control of the middle of the park early on; Hawkins had marshalled his fellow backs superbly; and as a consequence Swansea managed just a single shot on target in the entire first half.

As early as the quarter hour mark, North End got their first glimpse of 'The Washer Show' in action. Ross pounded down the right flank and crossed the ball towards Ingram, who flicked it on to the waiting Ham. After a little scramble with the keeper, the ball was in the net and the goal awarded. Or was it?

With North End almost back in position to kick off, Washer decided to consult his linesman - the upshot being the goal was disallowed, and a free kick awarded to the home team. North End had to wait some 20 minutes more before taking the 'legal' lead. A lovely through ball from the left to the diminutive Ham by McNab saw him turn his man in an instant and stroke home a shot that was his milestone 100th league goal.

Perhaps it was the welcoming half time mug of tea and slice of orange that lulled North End into a lapse of concentration early in the second half, as David Gwyther - the 'Swans' version of North End's Gerry Ingram - notched his 19th goal of the season to level the scores. However, the handful of 'Gentry' present only had to wait a few minutes before North End edged ahead again.

Mc Nab, bursting down the left, intelligently released Lyall forward with a superb pass. He, in turn, threaded a pass forward to Ingram who had no problem whatsoever in converting his 18th goal of the season.

After another 22 minutes of total business like control of the game, we arrived at the last minute. Cue Mr. Washer.

Some interesting facts and figures emerged following this game.

North End's last defeat was on 17th October, and were now unbeaten in 12 League games, taking 16 out of a possible 24 points. They were also the only club in the Third Division to remain unbeaten at home.

Things were certainly looking up it seemed...that was until Monday's LEP arrived.

A sad and pathetic story under the headline of, **"BALL RAPS PRESTON BOO BOYS"** led the sports page. Apparently David Hughes, having a run out in the reserves at Deepdale had been targeted by a particular section of the crowd and verbally abused throughout the match. It must have been a vicious, sustained and appalling experience as the young winger had declared that, *"I never want to kick a ball for North End again,"* immediately after the game.

After talking through the incident on Monday with Ball, Hughes retracted his 'no more' threat, but still handed in a transfer request. Ball said it perfectly for all the fans, when he told the newspaper, *"I strongly ask that those people who shout such abuse keep away from this ground in future. I don't mind criticism, but this kind of thing is not helpful in anyway. Hughes is probably the cleanest living boy in the club. He doesn't drink or smoke and trains very hard."*

Ball added that Hughes was down and miserable about the experience, but would pass the demand to the board for discussion as requested.

By Wednesday it was revealed that North End had enquired as to the availability of Bristol City's John Galley and Halifax Town's Bill Atkins - both centre forwards. They were available, but at a cost North End could not meet. The Keegan saga rumbled on too with still no reply from Scunthorpe United after North End's increased offer.

Last but not least, the North End board had duly granted David Hughes' transfer request following the shenanigans of the previous weekend during the reserve fixture. It was a very sad outcome.

The Walsall v Gillingham match, taken in by the North End team travelling back from Swansea had obviously provoked a few thoughts. Walsall won the game 3-0, so all week the North End first team squad had been playing against the reserve team - who graced the Willow Farm pitch in the style of Walsall. Only time would tell if the strategy would work, but at least North End would arrive at Fellows Park at full strength -the injury concerns to Ross and Ham clearing up by Friday.

In the event, North End never even boarded the coach. After heavy rain all over the country for days on end, there were postponements here there and everywhere. Fellows Park was one such place. The match was rearranged for the following Wednesday evening.

Plenty of time therefore for more off the field news to digest over the next few days. Southport, who had recently signed Frank Lee from North End were the first to put their hands up regarding David Hughes. However, it wasn't straight forward; struggling to make ends meet, 'Port manager Alex Parker wanted Ball to sanction a loan deal to help them out.

The increased £20,000 offer for Keegan was finally rejected by Scunthorpe, confident that all the publicity surrounding Ball's attempts to sign the 19 year old would ensure they would get their full asking price from one of the host of other alerted clubs. Several were apparently from the First Division.

Surprisingly, Ball revealed that he had received two five figure bids for his 28 year old midfield general Alan Spavin. *"These are both from Third Division clubs very impressed with 'Spav' after witnessing his performances this season. But I'm not prepared to let him go. As far as I am concerned he can stay here until the end of his career. He is a superb club man."*

The Walsall pitch was deemed playable after their manager, Bill Moore had the ingenuity to hire Warwickshire County Cricket Club's water pump to make the fixture safe. Moore added he was treating this game as the biggest test of the season as reports from his scouts and other clubs all had a common thread; Preston are the best footballing side in the Third Division.

Praise indeed!

Clive Clark was left behind as the coach pulled out of Lowthorpe Road and headed for the M6. He had pulled a groin in training, so Ball opted to select the unsettled David Hughes to make up the squad of 13.

The really interesting thing about this game, and from now on would be that North End's progress could be followed via local radio.

BBC Radio Blackburn had fired up its first few glowing valves the day before the Walsall game. As we well know, the station would cover all aspects of Burnley, Blackburn Rovers, Blackpool, North End and Bolton Wanderers (who were transferred to Radio Manchester after a couple of seasons).

It was like a dream world! North End - on radio - every match? You're having a laugh!!! But it was true! In a world of wired telephones in the hallway, no mobile phones, no internet, the newspaper and the teleprinter on 'Grandstand' were king if you needed North End coverage.

The North End correspondent was to be Norman Shakeshaft, who just happened to have the same position at the LEP.

If there were fans out there hoping for Hughes to take the field and be able to ram a huge performance down the throats of his ridiculous detractors...this was their night! The recalled winger played so well he was mentioned in both print and airwave dispatches.

Predictably, the green top to the pitch lasted about ten minutes before the final eighty were played out on a sea of mud.

Walsall performed very well. They gave a spirited display and held their own for 75 minutes. That was when good fortune tapped Hughes on the shoulder and said, "Go for it, son."

Receiving the ball on the right flank, Hughes went down the outside of the defence at pace, squeezing a centre in as he reached the by line; this despite the close attention of a couple of defenders. The cross was met by Ingram who deliberately back headed the ball toward the penalty spot where it was met hook, line and sinker by Lyall on the volley. It was unstoppable.

It was just reward for North End, as, despite Walsall's performance, they had been the better team. Spavin - maybe buoyed by the interest in him from other clubs - gave a midfield master class in the mud. In fact all the team contributed to what was a fine away win. From Hawkins and Spark at the back, barking out orders, prompting forward movement, through to the 'little and large' combination Ham and Ingram leading the forward line; it was a complete performance.

So 'complete' that Ball opened the post match press conference with, *"Weren't we great?"* He added, *"We were in a different class. Walsall played really well and it was difficult out there, but we've won 1-0 at a place where Aston Villa lost by three clear goals a few weeks ago."*

And so, what of Hughes? He was obviously delighted at the goings on and said, *"It was wonderful to have a hand in the win, but oh how I wish I had done it at Deepdale to prove to those supporters who barrack me that I have some talent."* That talent was witnessed by a clutch of on looking managers, including those from Ipswich Town and Wolves, namely Messer's Robson and McGarry.

Over the prolonged waterlogged weekend, the table had squeezed up a little at the top. Villa led the way with 36 points from 27 games, while North End were still fourth with 34 points from 26 games - level with Fulham and Bristol Rovers - a very handy position to be in as the going got tough on those wet, mainly clay pitches of old.

Clive Clark was the name still missing when the squad for the weekend home game against Chesterfield was announced. Essentially it was exactly the same squad who had fought and won in the muddy trenches of Fellows Park, which meant a home run out for Hughes - his first since the puerile barracking he had received from Preston's very own lobotomy cases. The thought was - why weren't these idiots ejected by the stewards during the game? After all it was a reserve fixture and they would have been easy to spot in such a small turnout...anyway, everybody was sure Hughes would be cheered on this time.

Ball was more concerned about Chesterfield. *"They are one of the best sides in the Third Division, and very big physically. They have several six footers in their team and it's going to be very difficult for us."*

It poured down again on Friday and right up to lunchtime on Saturday. This would be another game which would test North End's stamina, so soon after the energy sapping Walsall game.

All the approach roads to Deepdale were busy though despite the weather; indeed just over 14,000 turned up to witness what must have been the best day in David Hughes' footballing life so far. He was simply magnificent.

Right: David Hughes in full flow

The first 15 minutes or so of the game ebbed and flowed, surprisingly Chesterfield looking like they were not here to spoil the game, but to win it.

Ingram hurried an attempt following a Hughes cross and shot wide, but the visitors were creating some problems in the North End defence themselves and came close when Ernie Moss tested Kelly with a shot, the ball running loose in the area before being thumped away reassuringly by Hawkins.

David Hughes seemed to be everywhere; this time well encouraged and appreciated by the large crowd, he combined in a lovely exchange with Spavin, before he and Ingram tried to replicate the North End move that resulted in the winner at Walsall – his cross laid back to in-rushing Lyall whose 20 yard missile like shot went narrowly wide of the post with Alan Stevenson the Chesterfield keeper, hopelessly beaten.

There was a sense now that North End had assessed the capabilities of Chesterfield and were upping the ante. The pressure started to build and Ham went very close with a rasping shot on the fly from 25 yards which Stevenson failed to hold, the ball desperately cleared off the line by the Albert Holmes, the right back.

Hughes was popping up everywhere and on the half hour, surged down the right wing and delivered a great cross that was met by the leaping Ingram - the ball finding the net to give the striker his 19th of the season. A superbly executed piece of play.

The attacks continued. Spavin delivered a slide rule centre from a free kick which Ingram met with power, the ball arrowing just over the bar. Hughes centred to tee up Heppolette for a terrific volley which absolutely screamed 20 yards through the air only to rebound loudly and violently against the crossbar and away to safety, with Stevenson pawing at thin air.

This was an excellent display of football from North End. The pace of the attacks was fantastic. Ham tried a lob from 15 yards; even Hawkins forayed up field to try and lend further weight to the attack with a lovely glancing header that tested Stevenson, from a Hughes corner.

Ross, buzzing and hurrying down the right crossed and saw Stevenson, with one eye on the two oncoming forwards, drop the ball and hurriedly gather it before referee Jack Taylor blew for an infringement by Ham.

Half time arrived with North End 1-0 up, and cheered off the pitch.

Following the chance to get their breath back, Chesterfield started the second half brightly. A good chance fell to Moss but he shot wide. Hughes however, was still rampant. He had a point to make – and boy, was he making it!

Moving at pace, he cut inside leaving Holmes for dead, and unleashed a scorching drive that was just off target. A few minutes later he was at it again. Dribbling past two defenders with consummate ease, he set up Heppolette on the left, but there were groans of frustration as the midfielder's effort sailed harmlessly out of play.

Meanwhile Kelly had to have his wits about him, saving brilliantly as McNab misjudged a headed back pass. The momentum had swung Chesterfield's way for a little while and the crowd were on pins.

As the game drew to a close, with fans desperately checking their watches, Hughes created a final chance for North End to close the game out once and for all but the queue of Ross, Ham and Spavin all failed with shots that rebounded off the visitor's defensive barrier in quick succession.

The final whistle was met with both cheers and relief; Chesterfield had certainly given North End a game, but it was a fully deserved win.

There was only one candidate for Man of the Match....

The headline in the *Football Post* made for great reading. "**NOW NORTH END MOVE INTO SECOND PLACE"** it shouted to one and all. What a great day Saturday, January 30th 1971 was! The team were not for slipping away; they were in for the long haul.

Desperate moments in the Chesterfield goalmouth as North End launch wave after wave of attacks

February

Gillingham, Olympics, Walsall, D-Day, Transfer Talk, Barnsley, Brighton & Hove, Get Dawson!

On Monday, all the talk in the LEP was about when Alan Ball would have his hair cut again. The Chesterfield win was the 14th League game without defeat, the last being way back in October against Halifax Town. Ball had stated during the unbeaten league run that he wouldn't have his hair trimmed again until North End were defeated. So out of control was the mop, the wives of the North End Directors presented him with a bow to tie up his unruly locks..!

For their endeavours in producing consecutive wins in very heavy conditions, Ball was to reward the team with a three day break from their normal routine, taking them down to the Bisham Abbey Training Centre during the week to be nearer to the Gillingham ground for Saturday's fixture.

It was announced that coach Denis Viollet was to leave Deepdale behind too - but in his case to go and try his hand in management with Crewe Alexandra.

Meanwhile Ball and Peter Doherty were off to a couple of Central League fixtures that Monday night to check the form of John Byrom of Bolton and Geoff Strong of Coventry City, *"just in case of emergencies,"* explained Ball.

By Friday, North End were coming to the end of a quite different type of week. According to Ball, although the training had been a little tiring, everyone was happy and he didn't foresee any problems. Maybe they were in a good frame of mind because Ball had arranged for the squad to attend the Royalty Theatre in London's West End to see a performance of Oh Calcutta! on the previous evening.

The state of play was Gillingham were propping up the rest of the Division and North End were second top, as I desperately tried to tune in the whistling and whining old radio to Radio Blackburn to follow the game. This was the first real chance I had of trying the new service, and surely it would be a good news day. The format back then had no main commentary game. There was a round robin of reports every 15 minutes or so but a hasty link to the ground was made when any relevant goal went in.

North End followers were having the best of it locally. The other local clubs, Blackpool, Bolton Wanderers and Blackburn Rovers were in dire relegation straits in their respective Divisions.

Evening Post reporter Norman Shakeshaft was Radio Blackburn's man on the spot. Things began well. The first report from the ground after kick off revealed that although Gillingham were playing above their station, there had been no real worries in the North End defence to date. North End had been enterprising enough so far with no reward. Great! This was good fun...although not for anybody else who wanted to listen to the television or even have a conversation. The warble and twitter of the radio tuning circuit was *very* annoying!

Before the second 'cued' report, we had a "goal at Priestfield Stadium" moment from the studio presenter. Far from being excited, I found myself in dread and torment as I waited for Norman Shakeshaft to crackle through on the airwaves. I only wanted good news...

It was a goal for North End, thank goodness!

North End had increased the tempo a little since the previous visit to the ground, and had taken the lead with a well taken goal. Spavin had made a break down the right, and waited for Ingram to arrive in the penalty box before floating over an inch perfect cross which was met with some power by the big centre forward, the ball flying past the keeper.

What a good feeling that was as Shakeshaft handed back to the studio. And there was more good news when he turned up again for his second report. North End were creating more chances with Clark becoming more prominent despite the attentions of his marker. Ball had left the dugout on one occasion we heard, to remonstrate with the referee when Clark was sent airborne by the right back but no foul was deemed to have occurred in the officials mind. All good then; the next report was due at half time.

It duly arrived, and was again positive. Since the goal, Ingram had seen a header scrambled off the line, a Lyall volley had cannoned off a defender with the goalkeeper beaten, and Ham had seen two shots saved. At the other end the only slip of the day so far from the North End defence was an under hit back pass to Kelly from Hawkins which let Gillingham striker Brian Yeo in, but his shot slid wide. Things were well on track for another win....

The 15 minutes or so seemed to drag until Shakeshaft was summoned for his update. Things were still going swimmingly it appeared. North End had started the second stanza well and Gillingham were just firing long hopeful crosses into the box which were being exclusively dealt with by Hawkins and McMahon. As the update closed, Spavin fired yet another drive at the Gillingham goal, which was scrambled away by the keeper.

I was probably toying with my Shoot! League Ladder theoretically improving North End's position should other results go their way, when news of a goal came through. Immediately on pins, a sick feeling descended on me as Shakeshaft ran through the details of Gillingham's equaliser. They had brought their sub on after 67 minutes and he was apparently creating havoc. The player in question, Ken Pound, had delivered a perfect cross for the unmarked Yeo to head past the helpless Kelly. I didn't want to really listen to the rest of the report; I was gutted.

To take my mind off the trauma I seem to recall that I picked the heel compass out of an old pair of TUF Wayfarers, no longer interested in speculating with the league ladder. With still about 20 minutes to go, I had already forecast the worst outcome in my own mind.

The next visit to the Priestfield Stadium had me holding my breath as we were told that it was all Gillingham now, they had upped their game so much that Ball was out of his dugout again shouting at his team, as probably he, like I, saw the game slipping away. "North End are just about hanging on with just under ten minutes to go, back to the studio."

I already hated this new service I had dreamed about using!

I think I would rather have been hit across the face with a wet fish than have the inevitable, "goal at Gillingham" barked out at me from a studio somewhere in Blackburn. But here was that moment - I waited with baited breath. Please God, let it be a winner for North...before I could complete the thought Shakeshaft had already told us that Gillingham had gone into the lead. With around 3 minutes left, a shot had been only partially cleared by North End and it was the mercurial Pound who buried the rebound in the North End net.

I didn't wait for anymore. I turned the radio off, much to the gratification of my Mum and Dad. I now waited for 'Grandstand' and the teleprinter to complete the misery. Sure enough, the result clattered through, along no doubt with a few instant stats that only David Coleman could deliver and make bearable.

The *Football Post's* lead headline was, "**SHOCK DEFEAT FOR PRESTON.**" It had been three and a half months since I had read about a North End league defeat, and after reading through the match report again, I concluded things probably weren't so bad after all....and at least Alan

Ball would be ok for a haircut next week!

Aston Villa headed the table with 38 points from 29 games, Bristol Rovers were second with 36 from 27, North End third with 36 from 28 and Fulham fourth with 35 from 28.

By Monday the more considered report of the game was there for all to read. *"We played too much football,"* growled Ball. *"We were too nice. We were quite content to play around in midfield instead of going out and getting the second goal. I am sure Gillingham would have broken if we had scored another. All very pretty, but not what was needed in the circumstances"*

Monday also brought along something quite different North End wise - a Deepdale run out against the Great Britain Olympic XI. It was the first of a couple of friendlies arranged by the club over the next month. The second would be early in March against Danish First Division outfit Randers Freja.

Looking down the programme I can't find any names in the entirely amateur GB team that went on and turned professional apart from Paul Fuschillo. Indeed, this enthusiastic and willing team who held North End to 0-0 on the night had the odds heavily stacked against them at the 1972 Olympics.

While we abided by the letter of the Olympic law, some Eastern Bloc of countries declared all their teams as 'amateur' so sent what were basically their first choice international teams to compete in Munich. No surprise then, when Bulgaria knocked our lads out in the early stages.

There was a fight to get no less than six North End players fit for Saturday's home clash with Walsall. It was reported that Spark, Ross, Hawkins, Lyall, Clark and Ingram were being treated for a variety of injuries although hopefully most would be available for the match.

Ball, meanwhile had taken in a Central League game at Blackpool to view their 'for sale' list, but came away unimpressed. In fact he headed straight to a hot pot supper at The Sitting Goose at Bartle where he was a guest of the supporters' Phoenix Club.

Apparently he made a stirring speech to the members, and for the first time let slip that, *"There's a long way to go, but I have a sneaky feeling we'll win promotion."*

Ball's next trip out was the following evening to Cardiff, to watch, and apparently enjoy, the performance of Brian Clark, City's centre forward. The swing ticket hanging around Clark's neck of £30,000 was beyond North End's money box anyway, as Ball declared sadly, "It is a tragedy. Clark is an ideal 4-3-3 front runner for my requirements and impressed me with his first time shooting. He is just the type we need. But Cardiff's valuation is beyond us I'm afraid."

Immediately the playground speculation began. Ball had just bought Bobby Ham, so the obvious forward that Clark would theoretically replace appeared to be Gerry Ingram...strange, as he was the Division Three leading scorer!

By the eve of the Walsall game, there was good news on the injuries and illness front; only George Ross was still a doubt, the rest of the 'crocks' having responding to being thumped about on the medical room table by trainer and 'player mender' Harry Hubbick.

For all you weather and global warming geeks, the 13th February 1971 was very wet – a mixture of driving rain and hail on the back of a gale force wind, not the ideal weather for standing on the largely open Deepdale terraces. But, this was a special season, and sacrifices had to be made; so on went my Parka, and off I went to catch the bus, dismissing my Dad's, "You must be barmy going out in this" along the way.

Taking my place at the Kop end of the West Paddock, water was beginning to collect on the pitch in small puddles as Alan Ball was presented with his gallon of Bell's Whisky after being elected Division Three Manager of the Month for January. The rain continued, but the players duly ran out at five to three and all was set.

Walsall kicked off towards the Kop with a mighty breeze behind them, but it soon became evident that any hopes of a football master class such as the last home fixture against Chesterfield would have to be ruled out. With the conditions as they were this was a 'win any old how' game - I doubt the wet and frozen crowd would care too much about witnessing pretty football!

Within five minutes the pitch resembled a semi ploughed field, but North End soon settled into some sort of rhythm and the lightning quick Clark was soon outpacing his marker to win a couple of corners. With the gale blowing, Kelly was having trouble reaching the half way line with drop or goal kicks, and the North End midfield radar was askew as several passes failed to make the distance to or went wide of the intended recipient.

Walsall were finding the conditions a bit of a leveler, and despite North End having the bulk of the possession, the visitors had the best three chances of the half. With North End caught upfield, Jimmy Seal sped down the wing for the visitors. His low hard cross found the arriving John Woodward, who only had to slip the ball past Kelly to score but he mistimed his shot, and the ball tamely rolled to the grateful Irishman.

No sooner had the terraces recovered from that heart stopping moment, Walsall cut through the defence again. This time it was Geoff Morris wasting the golden chance, after being put in by a pass from Woodward.

Finally North End got a grip of the game and the quite brilliant Clark, causing consternation in the Walsall defence wherever he roamed, setting up a shot on goal for Ingram, which was blocked and another for Heppolette which was a good 25 feet too high to trouble the Walsall keeper.

Walsall tried again, and wasted yet another great chance to go ahead. Seal made an opening on the right and centred perfectly for Morris, unmarked in the box. As the crowd held their breath, Morris headed the ball straight at Kelly who once again couldn't quite believe his luck.

Half time arrived with the cold, wet home spectators a little agitated that their team hadn't really looked like scoring while often leaving the back door open for the visitors.

After my usual heartwarming polystyrene cup of 'dishwatter', North End started the second half in conditions that were actually getting worse. After a couple of minutes it was evident that Ball must have delivered a bit of a 'gee up' speech to his troops, as they appeared to be playing with more spirit and drive.

In the opening ten minutes or so, Lyall had a volley magnificently saved, Heppolette hit a screaming shot just wide and Ingram had another shot on the turn blocked by a defender. The crowd wasn't moaning now, they were loudly roaring the home team on.

With snow now falling too, the pitch was a freezing cold mud bath with players falling over everywhere, as did Ingram as he was just about to shoot at goal from around seven yards out. As the game wore on, the fans were becoming edgy as North End, literally ploughing forward, were caught out again by Seal and Woodward, the latter swiveling and hitting the ball past Kelly and into the bottom corner. A mighty gasp of relief was heard as the referee instantly ruled out the effort for offside and the North End fans and players collectively breathed again.

We were into the last 10 minutes by now and Ball decided to throw David Hughes on - a move rightly met by cheers - to replace the ailing Lyall who appeared to be limping. The crowd attendance had been announced as 11,540, not at all bad considering the conditions.

North End continued to be roared on forward by the faithful and with just three minutes left, Ham prodded the ball home from close range following an Ingram flick from a Heppolette centre. Needless to say the crowd went absolutely wild! The players were completely overjoyed, congratulating each other too.

What a win on what a day; to cap it off, someone on the bus with a transistor radio shouted out that Leeds United had been beaten by Colchester United in the FA Cup!

Getting home to the warmth of the coal fire was now a matter of urgency, but once there and gleefully reading how North End were now second in the table once again, just two points behind Aston Villa with a game in hand, made the whole wet, freezing experience so worthwhile.

The Monday following the Walsall game was 'D Day' or Decimalisation Day to give it its full title, when the United Kingdom converted its currency into units of ten from 12.

For weeks there had been trailers and programmes on TV educating people about the changes to come. We had done a fair bit at school too and it was pretty simple to understand. Not apparently for everybody though.....

My Dad had put his feet firmly in the 'it's a swiz' camp and deliberately used to raise confusing issues with like minded souls such as, "how can sixpence now be worth two and a half pence and two pence be worth five pence?" by conveniently mixing the old and new values. And the old favourite, "It was 240 pence to a pound, now there's only 100. Where's the rest gone?" always delivered with shrug of the shoulders and an expression like 'I told you so.' "I bet the shops in town are raking it in. It's like pouring money down t'sough," (pronounced 'suff' meaning drain - old Lancashire twang). There were many who agreed with him...

North End meanwhile had been busy following up their interest in Brian Clark, the Cardiff City centre forward. Ball, aware that City were short of funds had persuaded the North End board to let him call Jimmy Schoular, the City manager with an offer of £20,000. This was duly done, but immediately knocked back - for the time being at least. Schoular didn't actually say 'No' to the offer, but would not sanction any activity until City had completed their European Cup tie with Real Madrid, and was certain that their own promotion bid in the Second Division was well and truly over. This effectively ended Ball's interest.

By the end of the week, only George Ross was doubtful for the Barnsley away fixture, still carrying a knee injury from the Walsall game. His chances of passing a late fitness test were rated as 'doubtful'.

Ball was urging caution. *"Barnsley have won five of their last six home games and drawn the other, and will be no pushovers. But we will attack as usual and do our best to bring back the points."*

The weather had been very changeable all week and it was a very wet and muddy Oakwell as the players ran out for the pre match kick about.

Preston had a very large and vocal Gentry contingent present, cheering them on at every opportunity. Within minutes the surface had started to disappear and any football skill was at a premium. North End looked secure in these early stages, with McMahon - standing in for Ross - slotting in like the regular he had almost become.

North End were gradually getting on top, but as against Walsall the week before, their passing game was suffering in the heavy conditions. The play was generally slow and the pitch testing the fitness of the participants.

Spavin was at his reliable best, and dominating the midfield with shrewd passing and interceptions that gave North End control of the midfield. Behind him, Hawkins was commanding the visiting defence expertly and driving his team forward.

Clear cut chances were rare, but North End almost went one up as Clark set up Ingram with a great pass, only for the referee to blow for offside. Ham was becoming more prominent too; with two markers following him everywhere he still managed to put a decent shot just wide and have a penalty claim waved away.

The trend largely continued after half time, but while North End still lacked that characteristic bite, Barnsley had still not troubled Kelly after the first hour. Indeed it was the North End who finally took the lead on 65 minutes when the hard working Ham gained reward for endless effort with a shot from the edge of the box after a Clark pass. He hammered the ball home with his left foot, and was mobbed by his team mates for his trouble.

After a couple of further near misses engineered by the wholehearted McMahon, North End fell foul of their 'Walsall Sickness' and left the defensive back door open. Norman Dean found himself one on one with Kelly, but his effort was mistimed and Kelly pushed it out for a corner.

Going behind had sparked Barnsley into all out attack, and now they were beginning to look like the team that had won five of the last six home games. Hawkins was controlling his troops well, but was seemingly knocked out by a fierce shot by David Booth as the home team pressurised.

With Barnsley committed to all out attack, Clark proved a great outlet for North End as his ability to go on long, fast and mazy runs sometimes drawing a foul in the process, proved priceless.

It was one such foul after Clark had cut inside after a pressure relieving run, that ate up precious time as the ref booked the defender, and then Spavin 'considered carefully' his free kick options to eat up more seconds as the home crowd jeered. From the midfielders lob, Heppolette just failed to convert with a diving header.

Barnsley pressed forward again, but once more the willing Clark took the resulting loose ball forward, this time the eventual foul on him being serious enough to warrant trainer Harry Hubbick to signal that Clark was finished for the day. Hughes came on as substitute as the clock was inching forward to full time. Finally at around 5pm, (it was a 3:15pm kick off), the final whistle sounded and the points were clinched.

More joy to follow, too. Bury had beaten Aston Villa 3-1 at Gigg Lane, meaning we were top of the Division by virtue of goal average. Another fantastic day out!

Lancashire Evening

Football Post

No. 38,139 SATURDAY, FEBRUARY 20, 1971 3p

QUICK-FIRE GOWLING HITS SOUTHAMPTON OH SO HARD

SO SLICK

No praise too high for Illy —Boycott

PNE EARN VITAL WIN

Why soccer needs Big Brother

READ ALAN BALL ON PAGE 3

Brown move?

Fighting back

Goal down

Last laugh?

Booked

Shadows

Chorley fix Sunday date

Man. U. v South'pton

Thrilling climax to PNE game

Blocked

Birmingham v Bolton

Scoreboard

DIVISION 1

Arsenal	3	Ipswich	2
Blackpool	0	Derby	1
Crystal P.	1	Coventry	2
Everton	0	Liverpool	0
Leeds U.	3	Wolves	0
Man. Utd.	5	S'hampt'n	1
Newcastle	1	Tottenham	0
Nottm. F.	1	Burnley	0
[illegible]	[illegible]	Chelsea	[illegible]
[illegible]	[illegible]	[illegible]	[illegible]
West Ham	0	Man. City	0

DIVISION 2

Birm'gh'm	4	Bolton W.	0
Blackburn	0	Carlisle U.	2
Bristol C.	3	Millwall	2
Cardiff	1	Charlton	1
Leicester	3	Norwich C.	1
Middl'sbro	1	Sheff. Wed.	0
Portsm'th	0	Luton T.	1
Q.P.R.	1	Hull City	1
Sheff. Utd.	1	Sunderland	0
Swindon	[illegible]	Oxford U.	0
Watford	0	Orient	0

RUGBY LGE. CUP

Leeds	4	St. Helens	0
Castleford	9	Keighley	6

RUGBY LEAGUE

Huyton	0	Batley	0
W'ington	14	York	5

DIVISION 3

Barnsley	P	Preston	P
Bradf'd C.	1	Bristol R.	1
Bury	P	Aston Villa	P
Chesterf'd	P	Doncaster	P
Fulham	4	Port Vale	1
Gillingham	0	Rochdale	0
Halifax	4	Tranmere	3
Rotherham	2	Mansfield	1
Shr'wsb'ry	1	Plymouth	1
Swansea	1	Brighton	0
Torquay	0	Reading	4
Walsall	3	Wrexham	1

DIVISION 4

Aldershot	2	Exeter C.	2
Barrow	P	Grimsby	P
Bo'mouth	0	Southport	1
Chester	P	Crewe A.	P
Colchester	P	Newport	P
Lincoln	0	Notts Co.	1
Oldham	P	H'lepools	P
Peterboro	1	N'th'mpt'n	0
Scunth'pe	P	Darlington	P
Stockport	0	Southend	0
Workingt'n	3	Cambridge	1
York	0	Brentford	0

SCOTTISH DIV 1

Aberdeen	0	Rangers	0
Ayr Utd.	2	Hibernian	0
Celtic	4	Airdrie'ns	1
Cowd'nb'th	1	Clyde	1
Dundee U.	3	Kilm'nock	2
Falkirk	3	Morton	1
Hearts	0	Dundee	0
Motherwell	4	Dunf'mline	3
St. Mirren	0	St Johnst'ne	1

SCOTTISH DIV 2

Albion R.	P	Berwick R.	P
Alloa Ath.	P	E. Stirling	P
Clydebank	3	East Fife	0
Forfar	3	Queen of S	0
Hamilton	2	Stenh'muir	2
Montrose	P	Stirling A.	P
Partick T.	5	Brechin	0
Raith Rov.	3	Dumbart'n	0
Stranraer	1	Arbroath	1

LANCS COMB.

AMATEUR INTERNATIONAL

V. of Lune v Stafford

CENTRAL LEAGUE

Stafford v Fleetwood

PREMIER LGE.

RUGBY UNION

COUNTY CHAMPIONSHIP

Bourne'th v Southp't

T.V. SOCCER

FOOTBALL FINAL SCORES

AMATEUR CUP

PREMIER LEAGUE

THE 'POST' BEATS THE STRIKE AGAIN—SEE PAGE 4

Ball's reaction to being Division Three leaders was typical, and indicative of his professionalism. *"We need four more points to be certain of avoiding relegation. That's our first task."*

It may have been a little tongue in cheek, but his insistence that being top of the league only counted for something after the last match of the season made perfect sense. *"We are certainly not celebrating yet; there is a long way to go."*

There was a lot of celebrating at school though. As I have mentioned before my generation had never known such success, and everybody was buzzing about it.

The North End management were still flying around watching potential 'targets' as the transfer deadline day loomed. Ball had asked politely about Derby County's reserve centre forward, Frank Wignall, and asked again about Bristol City's John Galley, both enquiries being met with a polite 'No.'

With the away fixture at Brighton coming into view, getting the squad fit and ready was proving a headache, with Heppolette being sent home with gastro enteritis earlier in the week. Ball took a gamble and pushed him on the Brighton bus after the player reported an improvement. Clark recovered from a bruised shin, but Ross was still not ready. With a bit of luck, Ball would be fielding the same team that did the business at Barnsley.

With Aston Villa occupied in the League Cup Final against Tottenham Hotspur at Wembley, there was a chance to make the game in hand count. *"We are going to give it a real go,"* said Ball.

For me, this was another game to reluctantly follow on the new fangled Radio Blackburn 'Saturday Sport' programme, that had left me feeling queasy a couple of weeks before.

The first thing to note when the reporter made his pre match report was that it wasn't Norman Shakeshaft. It was obviously a local journalist, as although he was trying to sound positive about North End, he was bigging up Brighton even more.

After roughly 15 minutes, the first report of the afternoon was delivered to the small, but eager audience. Immediately I was put on edge again. I hated this service!

Brighton had made all the running apparently, and just a minute before the reporter had thrown the 'tell Radio Blackburn switch' John Napier had headed just wide of the North End goal following a long spell of Brighton pressure. Kelly had been very busy, due to the fact that North End's midfield was being overrun and unable to steady the ship. North End attacks were not mentioned. Oh dear.

He said he would update us later with further news, but I didn't really want him to come back at all!

He chimed back in at around the 30 minute mark. Obviously the pattern of the game had not changed, as he described a litany of Brighton chances and efforts on goal, mentioning North End only in passing and that Ingram had nearly scored 'against the run of play', when he intercepted a mistimed back pass to the Brighton keeper, only to see his shot eventually cleared. As he was signing off, there was a mighty roar, and shouting above the noise the reporter said that McNab had just headed a Peter O'Sullivan corner off the line and away to safety.

All this was making me very nervous. As the clock ticked around to half time, none of those dreaded 'Goal!' announcements had been relayed from the Goldstone, so I was becalmed when we were taken over to the ground for the half time report.

Things had continued much as before; Kelly making a spectacular diving save from a powerful 30 yard shot by John Templeman, then Kelly again - this time diving bravely at the feet of Bert Murray as the rest of the North End defence stood like statues, arms aloft appealing for offside. The dive had caused an injury to his right shoulder, which he had been holding on and off up to half time. North End hadn't played like promotion contenders to date; they were definitely under the cosh.

As the second half kicked off, the North End fans listening could only hope and pray that they got it together.

Then, on the 53rd minute, we were whisked back over the airwaves to the Goldstone. There was no goal jingle, so what could it be? That was quickly answered - the reporter gleefully reporting a home penalty. My heart sank.

Kelly and McNab had collided with winger Alan Duffy in going for a centre from the left. Without hesitation, the referee had pointed to the spot, much to delight of the home crowd. Preston's protests were still holding up the game but eventually the referee waved the players away and Napier stepped up to take the spot kick. The tension was enormous - and not just at the Goldstone!

There was silence, then cheers, then confusion. Apparently, Napier had shot low to Kelly's left, but the keeper had dived brilliantly to parry the shot. Napier moved forward and tapped the loose ball into the net, but for some unknown reason the referee ordered a retake. If I was nervous before, this was unbearable. They were bound to score now, weren't they? Absolute racing certainties!

This time it was Alan Duffy who placed the ball on the spot. He hit a hard shot...that cracked against the bar and away to safety! Yesssss!!!

On that note, the bemused reporter handed us back to the studio. Phew!

The next report was a little better. Brighton were not dominating quite as much as before, but the North End attack was definitely on a 'go-slow' this weekend. North End were creating the odd chance, but now coping with the home attack much better, as Brighton seemed to be tiring. Just over ten minutes to go, and if we held out, this would be a great point!

Before Radio Blackburn relayed the full time report from Brighton, the 'Grandstand' teleprinter had rattled the 'draw' result out, so I didn't bother with the radio any longer. I was feeling a lot better now as I awaited the arrival of the *Football Post*.

The most interesting part of the newspaper was the star *'2 Guinea Letter'* (which surely should have been changed to the *'£2.10 Letter'* by now...), in which a chap from Walton le Dale pleaded for North End to bring back the legendary Alex Dawson to solve the North End goal scoring 'crisis.'

Arguing that Dawson was only moved on in the first place, *"because of ex-manager Jimmy Milne's insistence on playing 'over square' defensive football,"* he declared that, *"lack of support and opportunity took the Black Prince's scoring touch from him - he didn't lose it,"* adding that now North End were attacking again under Ball, he would fit the bill perfectly.

"He will get all the opportunities he desires from the many crosses being supplied by Ross, Clark & Co., and I feel that Ingram would provide him with the same support that Alec Ashworth used to. Add Bobby Ham to pick off the half chances and George Lyall to crash home the long ones and I still feel North End would score more goals this season than we did in 1964, and that is what the fans want to see."

It must be said that Dawson was a fantastic striker for North End and even now is held in great affection by those who witnessed his no nonsense exploits and finishing, but his return was never really going to happen, despite the sentimental argument above. Besides that, the writer didn't state who he was going to leave out of the team.....

March

Randers Freja FC, Plymouth Argyle, Deadline Day, Bury, Rochdale, Rotherham United, Doncaster Rovers, Port Vale, Friends with Swindon

Before a ball was even kicked during March, I had a sudden 'crisis' to negotiate.

Good friends of my parents had invited our family to the wedding of their daughter on Saturday, March 27th. As the invitation was being relayed to them over a Sunday morning cup of tea, instantly I was saying 'Port Vale, home' in my head and nipping upstairs to check my North End fixture list.

With the Port Vale game now under serious threat, I gave the matter some thought over the coming days as how to enjoy both events – but at some stage I would have to ask my parents if they could approach the hosts on my behalf.

Having got a sort of plan together, I decided Mum was the best conduit to use in this situation. I went through it all with her and ended by saying, "and if the wedding timings go to plan as they say on this card, I will be able to be at both because you will be having drinks and things while I will be just sat around...."

I can't remember if my fingers were crossed behind my back, but they should have been. Mum hadn't exactly agreed, and was pulling her face a bit, but she hadn't disagreed either. I played what I considered to be my ace. "Well...can you ask them from me if it's ok because obviously I don't want to be rude...?" She said she would, so I just had to sit back and wait.

They all went out together one night per week, and I stayed awake that particular night so that I could ask if it was a good outcome for my petition. I sort of skirted around the subject, then asked. "Oh, I forgot to mention it," said Mum. "Sorry."

I must have looked very forlorn - I certainly felt it - but then Mum laughed and said, "They said it's alright, so you can go." Oh bliss! I offered grateful thanks and went to bed. It meant that all things being equal I would be a 'home ever present' this season. So, so selfish!

The first week of March saw a visit from Randers Freja FC from Denmark. It seemed like the North End programme editor had been browsing holiday brochures to find some inspiration as he billed Randers as, *"interesting newcomers to Deepdale from the fair and peaceful land of Denmark whose amiable people enjoy making friends and leading an active healthy life."*

Amateurs or not, this club had won the Danish Cup twice, appearing in the European Cup Winners Cup in 1968/69. They drew a crowd of around 4,000 – including yours truly – and suffered a 6-0 drubbing at the hands of their hosts. A first half hat trick from Gerry Ingram was followed in the second half by goals from Willie Irvine and two 'A' team hopefuls, Alan Lamb and a certain Alex Bruce.

The goal by Irvine was both vintage and poignant.

Vintage in the fact that, the once 'darling' of Deepdale rolled back the years by rounding the keeper and slotting the ball home with some panache. Poignant because within a few hours he was lined up to be loaned out to Brighton, and we would never see him in the Lilywhites shirt again.

Plymouth Argyle were the first League visitors of the month to Deepdale. George Ross had finally returned to contention and would have a fitness test on the morning of the game.

Old friend and now adversary, Bryan Edwards who was on the North End coaching staff under the previous regime, had declared his determination to prove North End wrong for sacking him before the reverse fixture at Home Park in late October. This time he was a little more complimentary. *"Preston are the finest side in the division, but I have given our lads a complete run down on every North End player, and we aim to stop them."*

The game was actually a story of total domination. In fact, although North End ran out 1-0 winners it could easily have been another 6-0 home win to neatly follow on from the Randers Freja friendly.

Ross passed his fitness test and took his place at right back for North End. The snow that had fallen over the past couple of days had melted but had left the pitch seemingly saturated and heavy.

Within minutes of the kick off, North End were controlling the game. A Clark centre towards the on rushing Ingram was magnificently pulled out of the air by former Arsenal, and latterly, Rotherham United goalkeeper Jim Furnell, now operating between the Plymouth sticks. That was just the start of it. Furnell was to have the game of his career!

A typical Lyall snap shot from the edge of the box had Furnell tipping the ball over the bar, and then a clever flick from Ham was prevented from entering the bottom corner of the net by the sprawling keeper. Two more wonderful stops from Clark and Ham were followed by a magnificent diving save after Ham had picked his spot with a well placed header, the ball being pushed around the post.

Lyall shot wide, Spavin had a shot blocked and Clark was within an inch of touching home a loose ball in the area. All this, and the game was only around 15 minutes old.

The magnificent all out attacking play had the crowd roaring, but Furnell's display was unbelievable and the crowd was in awe, and not slow to show their appreciation.

Spavin was put through by Lyall, but yet another remarkable save saw the move end. The one way traffic continued unabated and Ham smashed a splendid shot against the bar with Furnell, for once, caught on his heels.

Plymouth ventured down towards Kelly for the first time after around 30 minutes. The move petered out before it reached the penalty area and the 'Furnell at Deepdale Show' resumed after its short break. After a free kick, Spavin put Ross in with a chance and his first time shot from an angle was well saved by you know who. Lyall then blasted a free kick goalwards from fully 30yards, Furnell adjusting late, twisting and palming the ball onto the cross bar having seemingly misjudged the pace of the shot.

As half time approached, North End ended their obvious frustration when they took the lead. After Clark centred, the ball ran loose in the Argyle penalty area and an orderly queue of North Enders lined up to take turns at blasting it home. Heppolette, then Ham had shots blocked by sprawling defenders. Lyall then pounced and thrashed the ball goalwards, and following a deflection, Ham darted in to stab the ball over the line. Finally!!!!

The players leapt around showing their obvious joy, and the roar of the 12,000 plus crowd was long and loud. There was just time for another Furnell save before the referee blew for half time and a great ovation for the home team – and indeed, Jim Furnell.

The second half began, and the frantic pace of North End's game continued. Clark created a great chance for Ingram with a centre on the run from the left after a mazy run. Ingram did everything right, meeting the cross perfectly and heading downwards from close range. The ball was goal bound but Furnell somehow managed to get an outstretched hand to the ball to take the pace off, enabling a defender to clear off the line.

Shots and efforts on target by Ham, Spavin, Ham, Ingram, Ingram and Ham were duly repelled by the quite wonderful Furnell, and North End could just not find that second goal which would surely kill off Argyle.

As time wore on and Plymouth were obviously tiring, they started resorting to the rough stuff, David Lean seeing his name written in the referees' notebook for his attempt to remove Ham's leg. Indeed, Ham worried Plymouth right until the end of this game. He was too quick in thought and speed for them.

Another 1-0 win and despite the two points there was a general buzz of concern that for all that endeavour and enterprise, North End were only one defensive slip away from having their points haul halved. Ball was still frantically searching for a proven front man as the transfer deadline rapidly approached, but who would he leave out and was a new signing a guarantee of goals?

North End had a home fixture just a couple of days later against Bury. To enjoy this fixture I would have to endure a Monday at school. I was finding that as North End homed in on a promotion spot, my concentration at school was diminishing in proportion. And it certainly was on a Monday afternoon with a double dollop of Modern Maths to send you home confused and depressed.

Why oh why was that bastardised branch of the subject ever introduced? I was – and still am – pretty decent at conventional Maths, but this was beyond the pale...it has scarred my mind for decades. I just wanted 'times by' or 'divide by', but had to learn a whole new language and subjects, like 'Intersection' and 'Matrices,' at the same time being urged to forget all about the previous stuff I had learned with ease for years.

Thankfully, I have never known a day since I have left school where I have needed Modern Maths to survive. Conventional Maths? What do you think?!

I obviously survived that boring afternoon to take my place in the

Pavilion Paddock around the half way line as I recall. I had gone with a school friend, and spotted a couple of others inside the ground too. It was the biggest League crowd of the season to date; a touch over 17,000 and very cold and clear.

As if to celebrate this fact, North End started at a canter and went ahead with an early goal from Spavin. Moving forward, the Division's midfield maestro received a pass from Heppolette, beat one defender, performed a quick one-two with Ingram and gave John Forrest, the Bury keeper no chance with a great shot.

Bury gradually emerged from their half and put together a few decent moves, one which resulted in a glorious 25 yarder from Hugh Tinney, almost taking the North End net off its fixings as it sailed past the outstretched Kelly. Fortunately the goal was immediately ruled out for offside, and North End started again.

The pressure was building on Bury as the half wore on and it was no surprise when Clark netted and celebrated with some joy the 100th strike of his notable career.

Heppolette sent over a long centre from the right towards Lyall who left it to run onto Clark racing in behind him, about 15 yards out. Meeting the ball and swiveling in one motion, the wingers' shot crashed into the net leaving Forrest helpless.

The second half was a little more sedate, as North End went into coast mode. Ingram could have added to the score on a couple of occasions but didn't, and it was Bury who came closest to scoring when centre forward Tom White hit the post but Kelly managed to smother the rebound.

Hawkins had another fine game, directing his defensive troops superbly. It was now five games since North End had conceded a goal, and the captain was repeatedly displaying qualities that were worthy of a bigger stage. With Spavin, he formed the fulcrum of a team that was on the brink of something quite special.

The win took North End back to the top of the table, with 45 points from 33 games. Fulham were second with 43 from 33 and gatecrashers Halifax third with 42 from 34.

As the March 11th midnight transfer deadline neared, Ball had initially landed on Derby County as the place to find cover for Ingram and Ham. North End began the day with a fair degree of optimism, as Ball's persistence had seemingly paid off with Brian Clough agreeing to release Barry Butlin....until he changed his mind around midday.

Immediately, Ball initiated Plan B, telephoning Coventry City to enquire about their reserve centre forward, Billy Rafferty. City manager, Noel Cantwell was more receptive than Clough and agreed to meet Ball and his party half way at a motorway service station. A fee was quickly agreed, but Rafferty didn't particularly want to move north, so Ball saw this little avenue of hope closed off too.

With time running out, Ball called Bolton Wanderers and asked about the possibility of Roger Hunt being allowed a loan move until the end of the season. This was refused; and the same telephone call also ended any hope of John Byrom being allowed to move up the newly laid M61.

Further calls to Liverpool about young forward Jack Whittam, to Ipswich about Frank Clarke and Coventry City regarding Brian Joicey were all returned in the negative. With time running out, Ball convinced the board to increase the cash on the table to £40,000 largely to interest Wolves into releasing Derek Dougan, but this failed too.

The failure to land an additional striker was disappointing for all concerned, but it wasn't for the want of trying. Apparently Ball logged 124 calls during Deadline week in the vain search for a striker.

While the whole of football seemingly knew what Ball wanted during that week, he did however pull off what proved to be an extremely significant piece of business for North End on the quiet.

He convinced good friend and rival, the Doncaster Rovers manager

Lawrie McMenemy to part with John Bird, a 19 year old defender who had impressed him for quite some time. Bird was rushed across to Lytham St Annes and duly completed the move in time.

It would be the most rewarding £5,000 that Ball ever spent on a player.

Following the Bury home win, North End were due to check in at Spotland, Rochdale for the next fixture. North End fielded a full strength team, identical to that of the Bury match - the midweek doubts over Spavin's match fitness being cast aside during a pre-match fitness test.

For this 'local' clash, North End took lots of fans with them, the Gentry being prominent in both number and noise level. In fact, the ground was absolutely packed that day. A glance at the official programme revealed that a gate of around 5,000 was a fair average, this crowd would be officially recorded at 10,249.

Early exchanges from both sides were quickly forgotten as Clark streaked down the left wing as though he had been shot from a gun. Leaving full back Ronnie Blair flat on his backside, he crossed on the run into the box. The ball eventually fell free but Lyall's shot was a rugby league conversion.

It was though a tap had been turned on, both teams springing to life. Heppolette split the defence in two with a glorious ball for Ham to run onto; his shot hooked clear on the Rochdale goal line by Derek Ryder. At the other end, Denis Butler forced a good save from Kelly, as his hard drive from outside the box sped towards the Preston goal.

Clark was having a fantastic game and it was a corner delivered by him that led to North End taking the lead in the 18th minute. Floating into the box from the left, the Rochdale defence had several hacks at the bouncing ball but failed to clear it. Not so Heppolette, who strode forward to meet the loose ball and blast home from five yards.

It was due reward for North End, Ball's promise to play attacking football home or away was holding good.

Clark flew down the left again and right back Blair, already sick of the sight of him took the winger out waist high, bringing loud dissatisfaction from the Gentry and a lecture from the referee.

Rochdale were very tidy in their approach work, but it was noticeable as the half wore on that their moves were breaking down before reaching the North End box, perishing on the rocks otherwise known as Hawkins and Spark. With Ross and McNab snuffing out any threat from the Rochdale wingers, and indeed overlapping at every opportunity, North End were assuming control of this game.

After 36 minutes, North End almost increased their lead when Spavin slid a ball sideways to the on rushing Lyall who launched a trademark missile at the Rochdale goal, only a wonderful finger tip save from Tony Godfrey keeping the ball out.

Clark was still storming down the left wing at every opportunity, yet again the perfect outlet for the North End midfield. Within the space of five minutes, Blair took the flyer out three more times with increasing venom, the last proving too much even for the over tolerant referee, who promptly booked him much to the delight of the North End fans.

With half time approaching, Rochdale attempted to clear the deficit before their mug of tea and orange. For once the North End back line wasn't straight as they raised their arms appealing for an offside, David Cross was left to advance towards Kelly alone. Kelly quickly narrowed the angle and Cross's shot went inches wide of the post.

Rochdale started the second half well, Kelly rushing out of goal to smother a through ball from Ashworth, and Cross felt the force of a Hawkins tackle as he stormed through on North End's middle. A shot by Reg Jenkins then flew across the face of North End's goal with not a Rochdale soul in sight to convert the chance.

Ross broke the Rochdale spell of pressure by going on a superb forward sortie, easily beating fellow full back Ryder in the process. His cross aimed for Ingram was met in full, but went narrowly wide.

Heppolette, after starting a North End move, rose up to head Spavin's centre narrowly over the bar.

The game had turned and North End were now calling the shots again, and around ten minutes into the second half they increased their lead. It was a superb move involving Lyall, Ham and Ingram. Lyall and Ham worked a slick one-two on the edge of the box on the right. Ham advanced to the by-line and sent a firmly struck ball across the six yard box perfectly into the path of Ingram who stroked the ball home under the keepers diving body. The move was executed like clockwork. A superb effort; resulting in Ingram's 21st goal of the season.

Rochdale were pinned back now as North End went for the jugular. A third goal was almost registered as Spavin couldn't quite get a foot on a loose ball with the goal at his mercy. The one-two move, successful minutes earlier, was tried again this time Ham's cross being blocked for a corner. This was pulled back for the unmarked Spark to drill a marvelous shot just wide.

Further exchanges from both teams came to naught, but Rochdale finally got a consolation goal in the very last minute. From a corner, the unchallenged Cross headed home with somewhat ease, as though North End had already switched off...no doubt leading to a few words afterwards from Ball.

Nobody could really complain though. North End had displayed their promotion credentials once again, taking a grip of the game early on and not letting go.

Ball was pleased enough, post match. *"We were all over them and much the better team but only have two goals to show for it. We must be more ruthless in future."*

Quickly up next on the following Tuesday evening was another away fixture, this time at Rotherham United. This promised to be a tough fixture as The Millers were standing a creditable seventh in the table, losing only one of their 17 home fixtures to date.

None of the players on duty at Rochdale reported any adverse effects, so Ball went for the same squad for the third consecutive game. Assistant manager Peter Doherty said, *"I saw Rotherham a few weeks ago when they beat Bristol Rovers at Eastville, and they were very strong. We will do well tonight to bring back a point."*

He was quite right. North End did well enough to avoid defeat and bring home that point from a 1-1 draw.

In an immaculately executed first half performance, North End looked the 'real deal.' Such displays were usually in conjunction with an Alan Spavin master class, and this was no exception. He had put North End ahead in the 23rd minute, after Ross centre was guided into his path by Ingram. Pulling the match strings to his liking, Spavin was everywhere and creating everything. His passing accuracy was particularly notable; his creativity exceptional.

The Millers' game plan was to pump long balls into the North End box time after time, hoping that they would eventually get a connection or lucky bounce from one, but Hawkins, doing his best "Rock of Gibraltar" impression, saw to it that it was wasted effort.

Eventually they got their stroke of luck, courtesy of a North End error. A ball from Lyall to Ross struck the full back on the knee and broke to Jimmy Mullen, standing in the clear. He raced forward and beat Kelly with a low drive, the referee ignoring North End petitions that Rotherham centre forward Neil Hague was standing in an offside position.

Ball was content with the performance and point. *"We were different class,"* he said, adding *"but they did chase us like Red Indians in the second half!"*

Both the Mansfield and Doncaster managers, Jock Basford and Lawrie McMenemy were in the stands and agreed after the game that North End were the best team they had seen in the Third Division. Indeed with Doncaster Rovers due at Deepdale in a few days, McMenemy revealed he had been told several times, *"Stop Spavin and you can stop Preston."* Only time would tell if he could come up with such a plan by the weekend.

As Friday loomed, much was being made of the friendship - and keen rivalry - between Ball and McMenemy.

"I know as much about Alan as he knows about me," said McMenemy. *"I have made it my business to go through his team with a fine tooth comb and he will have done the same with mine. It will make for a good game even though we are at different ends of the table."*

Ball reiterated this opinion and said North End would have to be on their guard. *"We are a point clear of Fulham at the top with a game in hand, but anything can happen against a struggling team like Doncaster."*

With Ingram, Ham and Clark all recovering from bangs and bruises collected at Millmoor, Ball was expected to name an unchanged team yet again. With this team stability, North End were embarking on another run of unbeaten games, already this was up to seven after the surprise defeat at Gillingham in early February. The run consisted of five wins and two draws despite the Ball's concerns over missing chances to score the number of goals that the team's performances warranted.

The day dawned, and it was cold and damp with no doubt a heavy pitch. There was quite a throng making their way to the ground, and it was great to see and hear all the fans expectant of what was to follow.

And what a feast they were served up. It was the now usual start to proceedings by North End under Ball; unforgiving attack from the word go. The visitors answer to this was heavy tackling with a 'thou shalt not pass' attitude. This game plan was a moderate success for around 20 minutes, but it was never going to last against a team of North End's capabilities.

Heppolette was fouled, (surprise, surprise), as he attempted to work his way through a maze of flailing Rovers arms and legs on the right. The free kick was immediately handled blatantly, and from this Clark gained possession on the left, moved forward and passed inside to Spavin. His shot on goal was blocked, but the ball rebounded straight to Ham around 12 yards out who smashed the ball home much to the joy of a crowd irritated by the visitors tactics.

Within a few minutes, the lead was doubled. After yet another infringement, Hawkins took the free kick and floated the ball forward. Reaching Clark with his back to goal, the livewire winger somehow controlled the ball, and before it hit the deck, swiveled around and volleyed home a fantastic effort from fully 20 yards.

North End sensed the dam had been breached and launched raid after raid at the hapless Doncaster defence, further reward arriving around ten minutes before half time. A cross from Clark caused utter consternation in the defence as the ball was headed back and forth. Eventually, it was Ingram who had the presence of mind to calmly turn and head the ball down at the feet of Lyall who blasted the ball home in typical fashion from a few yards out.

Ham just fails to convert after being put through by an Ingram header with the Doncaster defence well beaten

Indeed, it could well have been four by half time as a Spavin cross was met by Heppolette on the run, but the keeper parried the ball away to safety. The whistle went shortly afterwards for half time, North End receiving a standing ovation.

Doncaster began the second half quite positively after a seeming rethink of their tactics. Two smart attacks resulted in good saves by Kelly, but North End soon hit back through Clark who shot narrowly wide after a rapid left wing raid.

The visitors were slipping back into their 'hoof the opposition' tactics as the half wore on, winning no admirers whatsoever. Anxiety was being caused by Ingram who was repeatedly beating the defence in the air despite the often illegal challenges he was enduring. Spavin produced a superb piece of skill, turning on a sixpence to instantly change the direction of play. His pass put Lyall through in an acre of room, but the midfielder wasn't thinking at Spavin's tempo and the opportunity ran to waste.

North End understandably waned a little after all their attacking endeavours, and Doncaster poked their heads out of their shells and attempted the odd move forward. Hawkins and Spark dealt with everything that came their way, with commanding performances. However Spark started to limp and was replaced by Hughes around 15 minutes from the end.

It wasn't long before the young flyer created the assist for North End's fourth goal. Spavin, Ham and Ross combined well in a rapid move down the right, the ball being fed to the waiting Hughes. After moving forward a few yards, he centred the ball perfectly into the path of Ingram, who with the minimum of fuss hammered the ball past the keeper to notch his 22nd goal of the season.

North End relaxed and saw out the last few minutes, exiting the pitch to loud cheers. They had delivered an excellent display of football to a crowd of just below 15,000.

My friend with his transistor radio fixed to his ear was keeping tabs on Fulham who were 2-0 down at Bury with about 15 minutes left. If this stayed the same it meant that we would be three points clear at the top with a game in hand. I'm glad to report it did. Happy, happy days!

March 26th was the eve of the aforementioned wedding, but the North End news was that both Spark and McNab were likely to be passed fit for the home game against Port Vale, after receiving knocks in the Doncaster game. Ball had issued a warning to both players and the fans.

"If you think Doncaster were rough, wait until you see Vale. They are very strong defensively and remember they beat us 1-0 last September."

Gordon Lee, the Vale manager, was very optimistic about the outcome after announcing an unchanged team. *"We expect to come away with something and the big match atmosphere could help my players."*

Needless to say, the exit from the wedding reception went smoothly, I slid away after thanking all concerned - the only drawback being I was overdressed somewhat for watching football at Deepdale. Not to worry; my Dad slipped me a 'a few bob' extra and told me to go and sit in the stand after I had explained all this to him.

It was a lovely day; one of those where you can actually feel the warmth of the spring sunshine when it appeared from behind the clouds. I took my place in the West Stand in another large crowd, this time turning out to be around 16,500.

It may well have been a lovely day but it was a horrible game. Vale adopted an aggressive defensive policy, and if they couldn't stop North End's attempts at enterprise with fair play, they had no hesitation in using foul. Gordon Lee got it wrong. The big match atmosphere took his team to a new low, and those who had paid certainly let him know about it.

North End had to be given some credit. Despite hardly ever getting out of the blocks, they persevered in the face of blatant intimidation to finally get the victory their bruised bodies so deserved.

The winning goal came on 74 minutes. McNab centred the ball from the left wing, with Ham completely and utterly selling a dummy to the Vale defence by allowing the ball to go through to Ingram, immediately behind him. Ingram calmly slotted the ball past the advancing keeper to bring loud cheers from the terraces – relieved that decent football was probably going to win in the end.

Ball revealed after the game that some of his players had requested at half time that they be allowed to respond in kind to Vale and get 'stuck in', but he flattened that suggestion, telling them to persist with football.

Indeed he was fuming at Vale's tactics. *"Everyone asks for entertaining football these days, and when we try to provide it, my lads are in danger of being badly injured. The Vale players were labourers."*

It was a very frustrating day. Another win, but the game destroyed as a spectacle. I suppose I should have been grateful though – in that I didn't have to watch Vale every week!

Early in the following week, Ball answered a Swindon Town S.O.S. call.

A Testimonial game for two of their stalwart first teamers, John Trollope and Roger Smart against Stoke City had to be cancelled at the last minute due to Stoke having to replay their FA Cup Semi Final against Arsenal in midweek.

Swindon manager Fred Ford, a personal friend of Ball's, asked if North End would travel to Wiltshire to help out, and was delighted to hear that they would. Besides helping out a couple of long serving professionals, Ball saw this as an opportunity to give some of his first team squad and fringe players a decent run out. In fact, before that game, a celebrity match was held with Ball and his assistant Peter Doherty both taking part, giving the North End team the added delight of seeing their bosses star in the 'Old Pro's XI'.

The North End players duly won their game 2-1. The match was played at league pace, with no tackles with 'feeling' allowed and was 30 minutes per half. It gave Wilson, Stewart, Patrick and Bruce the chance to get some air in their lungs; Bruce in particular very impressive.

As the month closed, the top of Third Division table showed North End leading with 52 points from 37 games played, Fulham next with 48 from 38, Halifax Town with 45 from 38 and Aston Villa with 45 from 37. The little breathing space at the top would be most welcome as this wonderful season was reaching its crescendo.

In just 31 more nerve jangling days North End had to play their remaining nine games. April - which included Easter - would consume seven of these, starting with a difficult away trip to Bristol Rovers. Never before or since has a North End season consumed me as much as this one did.

All this excitement so far; and now a final grueling lap...

April

Bristol Rovers, Tranmere Rovers, Reading, Bradford City, Mansfield Town, Aston Villa, Wrexham

April started with news that wasn't welcome. Alex Spark was likely to be missing from the squad travelling to Bristol Rovers, as he was suffering from a chest infection. John McMahon and John Bird were touted as the possible replacements, the latter having impressed in his handful of Central League games since signing from Doncaster Rovers on deadline day.

Indeed it was Bird who was given the nod just before kick off in this 'must not lose' game.

Tuning in to Radio Blackburn, Norman Shakeshaft mentioned in his preamble that BBC Match of the Day cameras were present at Eastville to record the game. This immediately struck fear into me - as previously noted, we never played seemed to play well in front of the cameras!

Rovers set the early pace, but before too long North End were into their flow. Cheered on by the loyal "Gentry" North End came close to scoring after a Spavin free kick from around 25 yards. The unique 'falling' or 'double' wall technique was utilised to almost perfection as Dick Sheppard, the Rovers keeper, just got a hand to the ball at full stretch.

Both sides were 'going for it', with Clark being roundly booed by the home crowd every time he touched the ball. He was having a real tussle with Rovers right back, Phil Roberts, but still remained North End's most potent forward.

New boy John Bird worryingly went down with an injury, but after receiving complex treatment from trainer Harry Hubbick - he was doused with cold water - he resumed.

The defences remained on top throughout the first half, with both teams cancelling each other out all over the pitch. North End had failed to take advantage of a strong breeze behind them as the half ended just as Spavin floated a free kick into the Rovers penalty box.

Rovers had the first opportunity of the second half. Ray Graydon had gained possession and moved forward towards the goal, but completely mistimed his shot and Kelly saved easily.

Lyall and Clark provided Ham with North End's first real chance; the left winger centred, Ham swiveled around and his shot on the turn was kicked off the line.

Interestingly, Ball had reverted to a 4-4-2 formation, which one assumed indicative of how precious he regarded getting something... anything - from this game.

Ken Stephens ran down the left for the home side, beat Hawkins and crossed, only to watch the ball go across the face of the North End goal harmlessly. Nevertheless the warning signs were there as Rovers increased the tempo of the game.

With 25 minutes left, Ball eventually - after a few sharp words with the ref - sent on Hughes for the limping Lyall and surprised everyone by reverting to 4-2-4, in effect gambling everything in an effort to gain victory.

This inevitably left room for the Rovers midfield to operate and indeed increase the exposure of North End's back line. Chances fell to Graydon and Bryn Jones in quick succession and the away fans were definitely biting their nails. Bird was having an excellent day under the wing of

Hawkins and these two provided steady reassurance whenever they were involved. Hawkins was becoming a real hero for North End as the pressure of this wonderful season reached its climax.

Clark eventually got a huge roar of approval from the home fans...his running battle with Roberts finally earning him a booking for dissent.

As time ebbed away, Spavin became dominant in midfield, foiling the inventive runs of Graydon on several occasions. Indeed, a North End breakaway near the end nearly earned the maximum reward for the visitors. The ball went out for a corner on the right side and Clark antagonised the home crowd once more by slowly jogging the full width of the pitch from the left to take it. Initially the ball was cleared but was returned with interest by Clark, leading to a flick on from Ingram just eluding Heppolette.

Ross and McNab had also shown admirable composure on a busy day, and it was the former who played himself and North End out of trouble just before the final whistle blew.

Definitely a point gained by the Lilywhites, and a real 'find' discovered in John Bird.

At the final whistle, Ball ran onto to the pitch and hugged each of his players as they came off. *"We could not play any brilliant football because of the strong wind and hard ground,"* he said, *"but we were magnificent, and we have now ended all Rovers hopes of going up.*

"My centre half and skipper, Graham Hawkins was superb and must be worth £150,000, while John Bird who I signed a few weeks ago for only £5,000, is already worth £20,000.

"It will be a tragedy now if North End don't get promotion after this performance."

Tranmere Rovers were the next visitors to Deepdale, and Alex Spark was still struggling to shake off his chest infection as the week progressed.

Ball rated his chances as 50/50. Having to replace significant defensive players at this stage of the season was on his mind, but he declared himself pleased that Bird had played with such control at Bristol.

Mathematically, North End still needed nine points to be assured of promotion, and it wasn't going to be easy with the fixtures ahead being quite difficult.

Easter Saturday dawned and as I recall it was a cool but glorious Spring day. Deepdale was absolutely bustling, with lots of people queuing at the turnstiles, the attendance eventually counted at 17,382. Quite remarkable really for a Third Division fixture, and even more remarkable considering where the club was just a year before.

Spark wasn't risked, and Bird kept his place alongside Hawkins, meaning that North End were unchanged.

North End attacked from the off, dominating the early exchanges. Spavin and Lyall soon started running the middle of the field, creating chances for both Ingram and Ham in quick succession. Frank Lane in the Tranmere goal was having a busy time, and when Ham turned provider by crossing for Ingram he was tested to the maximum by the striker's fierce header.

The game was being played out almost entirely in the visitors half, but the ball just would not go in for North End. On 23 minutes, McNab overlapping down the left with great regularity, centred towards Ham, whose header was cleared close to the line by a defender.

Bird ventured forward at a corner and saw a volley go close, and then Clark and Heppolette combined well on the left, forcing a corner. Clark delivered this well, but the move broke down and North End were seemingly becoming as frustrated as the crowd. On 35 minutes, Ham missed a 'sitter' blazing over the bar from just 5 yards following a glorious through ball from Heppolette.

Luck would change for the home side just before half time when the

Ham incredibly misses from short range in the home game against Tranmere Rovers

ever industrious Heppolette rushed into the box to meet a well placed free kick from right back Ross. The goal was due reward for the midfielder who had been the star of the North End show so far.

A late and rare venture towards the North End box by the visitors came to nothing as McNab coolly took control and fed the ever lively Clark charging down the wing. Ken Beamish, the Rovers centre forward performed a scissors tackle on the winger, resulting in a very entertaining lecture from roly poly referee Mr. Kirkpatrick which took us to half time.

Just before the restart, the half time scores went up. Letters A, B and C were the key ones on that day.

'A' - Gillingham v Fulham stood at 1-0. 'B' – Rochdale v Halifax Town was 0-3, and 'C' – Shrewsbury Town v Aston Villa was 1-0.

That was enough to raise cheers from the crowd, although in my mind Villa were becoming also-rans. It was Fulham and 'on the blind side' Halifax Town that appeared to have some momentum.

Soon after the restart Bird headed a McNab cross just wide and within a minute was tidying up a loose ball just outside the home penalty area.

He seemed like a real godsend – what a signing he was!

All the creative football was coming from Preston; combinations, solo runs, shots on goal. Tranmere's attack was non-existent but it was the old, old story of not converting decent chances.

As the game entered the final straight, news filtered through that Fulham were now winning at Gillingham, so to keep the status quo we needed both points. Ingram took a bad knock, but couldn't shake off the pain, limping to the sanctuary of the dugout a few minutes later.

Hughes came on, and in the final minute, crossed the ball when perhaps it would have been wiser to hold on to it and run down the clock. The keeper thumped the ball away down the middle of the pitch and past a badly out of position John Bird, who had been supporting the attack. It found Beamish, who moving swiftly forward, shrugged off an apparently injured Hawkins, and slid the ball past the advancing Kelly into the corner of the net, instantly ruining Easter for the 17,000 North Enders present. There was just time to kick off before Mr. Kirkpatrick flamboyantly ended proceedings for the day.

Fulham came back to beat Gillingham 3-1, Halifax won 3-0 and Villa went down 2-1. North End remained top, but now only by the virtue of goal average.

Agreeing that North End should have played safety first tactics at the end, Ball was just as concerned about the injury roll call. *"We could afford to drop a point; after all, half a loaf is better than none. But Ingram, Heppolette, Hawkins and Lyall all took bad knocks."*

All of this certainly increased the tension - definitely for the fans, and I suppose for the team too. With no football on Sunday's in the 70's, save for during the odd miners or electricians strike, Ball and his backroom staff had just those 24 hours to get those injured players back to match fitness. Two games in two days beckoned; Easter Monday at Reading and Tuesday at home to Bradford City.

As a fan, it was impossible for this season not to be on your mind almost all day long. It was the topic of conversation everywhere, and with North End faltering as Fulham and Halifax seemingly got a second wind, everything was up in the air now when only a couple of weeks ago we seemed certain of promotion. Had we peaked too early?

Easter Monday's events cranked up the pressure to unbearable heights with North End crashing to their first defeat since February 6th. In a game described as 'the same old story' in terms of chances created and not taken, they went down 1-0 at Elm Park.

The good news at the start was that the Harry Hubbick 'magic' - probably involving water - had worked yet again, and the injured foursome took their places on the pitch. That was really it as far as the good news went, unless you want to throw in that all too familiar first half domination without reward.

It was getting quite ridiculous. How could a team be so superior but not take their chances? It wasn't as though the strike force was impotent; Ingram was the leading scorer in Division Three, and Ham was almost as prolific!

Time and again, Preston's creativity was a class above their Berkshire hosts, and it carved open a mass of goal scoring chances. How Ingram, Ham, Lyall, Spavin and Clark must have rued the fact that their guns only fired blanks when it mattered most that Easter Monday.

Reading upped their game in the second half, but Preston contained them well. Perhaps though, they sensed that North End just weren't going to score and would give it a go, the best way a lower placed team could. That was usually with lots of enthusiasm and lucky breaks. And sure enough with just eight minutes left, both of those things came together and disaster struck for North End.

Hawkins appeared to have stopped Les Chappell in his tracks after the Reading forward hopefully chased a long clearance. The ball somehow broke away into the centre of the penalty area, where Bird was patrolling, and expected to execute an easy clearance. But he slipped, completely missing his kick, thus inviting Dick Habbin to slide the ball into the net. He did so with some aplomb, and that was that.

Ball was going to have to crack the whip, as it seemed that the pressure of spending the best part of nine months around the top of the table was starting to show. The breathing space North End had earned for themselves a couple of weeks ago was evaporating very quickly, now it was Fulham who were a point ahead, and seemingly bang in form. North End still had those couple of games in hand, but there had been a four point swing around towards Fulham in a matter of days.

Tuesday. Another day, another match. North End now had to deal with another lowly club, Bradford City, at Deepdale. Surely nothing could go wrong this time...?

The good weather continued, and so did the number of people flocking into Deepdale - just under 19,000.

You couldn't fault the North End effort. From the kick off the style of play was fast and furious and nobody was left in any doubt about their intentions.

They went ahead early. Spavin set the ball up beautifully for Ross overlapping at speed down the right. His centre was perfect, Ingram knocking the ball down for Clark whose shot was blocked by the keeper. The ball then ran to the ever alert Ham, who prodded the ball home from around five yards.

Then it was the create, dominate and miss your chances pattern of play all over again, which clearly frustrated sections of the crowd. Perhaps teams saved their heroics for the North End game, but it was becoming a worry.

Spark, returning to the team in place of Bird who had broken his nose at Reading, was unfortunate not to score on two occasions; Lyall had a shot brilliantly saved then sent another piledriver inches over the bar.

Other misses were debited against Heppolette, Ingram, Hawkins and Ham.

The crowd was strangely subdued though. Perhaps they, like me, a real Jonah in these situations, were thinking that while we only had a one goal lead, on current performances we were wide open to be caught napping again.

Lo and behold, that's just what happened – yet again!

Graham Oates, the City centre half but playing as a forward, headed home from close range after a cross from the left courtesy of Bruce Bannister. Oates had troubled the North End defence all evening and the warning signs had not been heeded.

As time wore on City became more desperate as North End continually probed, and turned it into a more physical game. Preston were stopped at every opportunity largely by overzealous challenges. However, it was enough and the delighted Yorkshiremen jumped up and down at the final whistle. Cue much moaning and groaning from disgruntled North End fans.

Ball switched on the reverse psychology button for the press after the game, fiercely defending his players. He always did this, protecting them from outside criticism when the need demanded. He claimed not to be downhearted but pleased.

"My players are men and they will do it for me. If that game had been a boxing match, it would have been stopped in the first half to stop Bradford from receiving further punishment.

"We sliced them apart time and time again, and created enough chances to have sewn the game up in the opening ten minutes.

"I know we did not take advantage, and this is something we will work on. We are the best team in the Third Division and we could afford to drop a point tonight. After all, it means we are a point nearer to

promotion."

You certainly could not criticise Ball in the way he was always publicly backing his players. He ended his positive stream of comments with, *"We have lost only six matches in the division all season. I rest my case."*

The following evening third placed Halifax Town, the team that just wouldn't go away, drew 2-2 away at Shrewsbury. So, with the Easter programme over, Fulham were top with 55 points from 42 games played, North End second with 55 from 41 and Halifax Town third with 50 from 41.

As the holiday from school flew by far too quickly, rumours were doing the rounds about how the North End players were happy to stay in the Third Division earning nice bonuses under the Ball regime, rather than being challenged in a higher section. This was palpably dismissed by the manager as the Mansfield Town away game neared.

"All the lads will be offered improved terms and their contracts reviewed if we achieve promotion, so it isn't an issue," he told the LEP.

He was understandably more concerned about several players battling to shake off injuries – indeed, most of the team were nursing something or other.

It was a cool and windy day in the East Midlands, as North End kicked off at Mansfield. The pitch looked a little ploughed in places and very bouncy. Ball fielded an unchanged team after all the injury scares of the previous week, which was a positive at least.

It was Mansfield who asserted in the early exchanges, and it was quite obvious the bumpy pitch was not going to assist North End's passing game. After just a few minutes, North End were dealt a body blow when Ham seemed to have damaged his leg in some way and was limping gingerly. Harry Hubbick came to his assistance, doused the leg in cold water, but even that had no effect. Wilson trotted on as substitute as the forlorn Ham was guided away by the trainer.

McNab and Lyall combined well to put Clark through, but he was stopped just as he was about to shoot and the ball was cleared. Football was a difficult game to play on this pitch, but the home team, obviously wise to this, were pumping crosses into the North End box from the wings at every opportunity.

It was from such a move that they took the lead in the 13th minute when Dudley Roberts headed past Kelly following a cross from the right by full back Sandy Pate.

North End huffed and puffed but Mansfield could see a chink of light and looked the more likely to score again. Spavin continually probed the home defence searching for the weak spots, but with Ingram now visibly limping and no substitute left, it was going to be an uphill battle.

In the very last in minute of the half, it was effectively game over. After a Hawkins header from a North End free kick had been saved by Rod Arnold in the Mansfield goal, the ball was quickly moved forward by the home team. Right winger David Thompson crossed the ball over and a brilliant flying header by that man Roberts left Kelly looking like a statue.

It was certainly all going sadly wrong for North End, 2-0 down and a developing injury crisis.

It would need a miracle to salvage anything from this game, but after the break at least we witnessed some construction in North End's game which led to the odd chance. It did seem though that with a limping centre forward, a very bumpy surface and being 2-0 down, North End would have rather been elsewhere.

A breakthrough of sorts came in the 72nd minute when Ingram defied the odds and headed home a Heppolette flick on from a McNab free kick. This signalled an increase in the North End tempo, and progress was made.

Spavin and Hawkins were becoming very vocal in driving North End forward. A Wilson cross created havoc in the home defence before the ball was hoofed to safety; then Lyall and Heppolette both had shots blocked in quick succession.

The clock was running down and with Ball and Cox animated in the dugout, North End pushed higher up the field in an all out attempt to rescue something from the game.

Heppolette went close again with a header and Spavin's floated free kick was just too high. Ross and McNab were raiding down the flanks too, but this tactical gamble would have a price to pay.

As the game entered the final minutes, Mansfield seized their opportunity.

McNab went down in the Mansfield box and claimed a penalty, but the ball was kicked clear. Thompson was on hand to steam through a massive gap in the middle of the North End defence, and drawing Kelly forward, slotted the ball home firmly.

Game, set and match.

Ball gave his usual 'reserved for defeats' upbeat response to the press after the game. Asked about North End's failure to get back into winning ways he said, *"Let's look at this from a different angle. If Dudley Roberts had been injured for most of the match and their other main striker had been taken off the field what chance would Mansfield have had of winning?*

"My lads fought like tigers against the odds and I was proud of them. They grew in stature and had Mansfield worried after Ingram's goal."

The news that Fulham had been held to a goalless draw at home to Shrewsbury was perhaps the most welcome and comforting news of a difficult day. Halifax Town had won though, beating Chesterfield at home 1-0.

This meant that the Third Division table now saw Fulham lead with 56 points from 43 games played, North End had 55 from 42 and Halifax Town 52 from 42.

Halifax just wouldn't lay down and die. They seemed to be getting positive results every week, while North End were now grimly hanging on. And with the prospect of North End having to face up to Villa and Fulham within the next fortnight, every North End fan was now having their nerves well and truly shredded.

Perhaps we should have taken a moment to reflect that things might not be so bad; after all it was almost exactly a year ago since we were bounced unceremoniously out of Division Two with seemingly no hope of progress ever again...

The other big football talking point of the weekend was West Bromwich Albion's surprising win at mighty Leeds United. A controversial goal, with an Albion forward seemingly acres offside was allowed to stand and cost Leeds the Division One top spot. Looking back now, this was a pivotal moment in both Leeds United's and Arsenal's season, as the Gunners never looked back once they had gained that top spot; eventually claiming 'The Double.'

April was throwing up games like they were going out of fashion; Aston Villa at Deepdale were next in yet another *must-not-miss-can-hardly-watch* occasion.

Friday's LEP caught the mood with a big back page spread on the match. Leading with **"BALL POSER AS TENSION MOUNTS,"** we were told that Gerry Ingram's chances of being fit were at best remote and worst still he was probably out for the season after having to limp through the Mansfield game with an ankle injury. This was dreadful news.

This match, between these two old and famous clubs was one of the most vital in North End's history, and our leading scorer was crocked! There was better news on his strike partner, Bobby Ham; he had recovered from a pulled muscle and would likely play. Ball named a squad of 16 - including Ingram - and would only decide on team and formation 30 minutes before kick off.

He had a simple message for the fans going to the game. *"I have just one request to the Gentry and all the fans who have helped us so much this season. Keep cheering us on!"*

April 24th was one of those damp days, with a lot of heavy cloud. But I could think of nothing else except North End v Villa from the moment I opened my eyes.

I probably went through my ritual as usual – a game of football on the road at the side of our house with some friends, then with lunch it was 'On The Ball' with Brian Moore on ITV, switching over quickly to catch BBC Grandstand's Football Preview with Sam Leitch. Then phone my school pal on the (hard wired) hallway phone to agree where to meet at the ground. I so, so wanted North End to win...

It wasn't to be. It was a 0-0 draw. But what an absolutely epic 0-0 draw!

Ball's final team selection was somewhat controversial. He dropped Lyall and, much to everyone's surprise started with Wilson and Bird. He went with:

Kelly, Ross, McNab, Bird, Hawkins, Spavin, Heppolette, Wilson, Ham, Spark and Clark.

Deepdale was buzzing as Villa kicked off, but the early inroads were all in the home teams favour. North End won a couple of free kicks which came to nothing, and were using Clark's left wing to good effect. He and Ham combined well teeing up the on running McNab whose shot was dealt with at the second attempt by John Dunn, the Villa keeper.

Villa were conceding quite a few free kicks around their penalty area and before too long, North End tried their 'Falling Wall' party piece to the home crowds delight. There were huge groans of disappointment though as Spavin's shot curled inches past the left hand post.

A foul by Charlie Aitken on Wilson led to yet another North End free kick just outside the box; Ross's centre being headed wide by Heppolette.

At last Villa came forward and Chico Hamilton raced onto a good pass down the right, only for the ever dependable Ross to execute a timely intervention as Andy Lochhead lurched close.

By now the pitch was cutting up badly and both teams were finding the conditions difficult. Villa, seemingly happy to concede possession, were now hitting North End swiftly on the break, only interceptions by McNab and Bird maintaining the status quo.

It was Bird who came to the rescue again after Hawkins mistimed a leap that had let in Hamilton only six yards out, sliding in with a tackle before the Villa playmaker could pull the trigger.

Willie Anderson then hared down the left wing for Villa and got over a great low centre which was met well by Lochhead but Kelly was well positioned to save.

This game was definitely worthy of higher stature as both teams continued to play great football. For the first time in quite a while Hawkins and Bird were being made to work very hard in the heart of the North End defence. Refreshingly Villa had come to play football, not kick lumps out of North End.

Spavin was having a superb game in the middle of the heavy pitch, working tirelessly and it was his deadly accurate cross towards Heppolette and Clark that forced the Villa keeper to drop the ball under pressure, gathering it in only at the second attempt.

The whistle went for half time and everybody was wondering just where the time had gone. It had been absolutely enthralling.

I couldn't really disagree with my friends who both thought that whoever got the first goal will end up winning. We were just hoping it was going to be us, especially when we learned that Halifax Town were winning 1-0 at Brighton and Fulham were drawing 0-0 at Doncaster...

Lochhead engineered the first move of the second half as he quickly went to chase down a through ball, leaving a couple of North End defenders in his wake. His cross into the box was calmly trapped by Bird who set off another North End move.

Ham found himself in some space at the other end but shot just wide, and a cross by Wilson was cut out by the keeper. It was end to end, and the home fans breathed a huge sigh of relief after a misunderstanding between Kelly and McNab at a short goal kick. Hamilton tried to gain possession and with Kelly stranded and the goal at his mercy, the ball tantalisingly ran out of play.

Around the hour mark, North End upped the tempo after a touchline barking from Arthur Cox. A cross from Wilson was brought down quite superbly by Spark whose fierce shot may have earned full reward but for a deflection off a cowering Villa defender. The resulting corner led to a frantic melee taking place in front of the Villa goal, and with no North Ender able to apply the final touch, the ball was cleared.

North End powered forward again. Spavin and Spark combined well before the latter put the speeding Clark through down the middle. The winger rounded one defender before passing sideways to Ham on the edge of the box. He in turn side stepped Brian Tiler, but his shot was blocked en route to goal by another defender.

This was simply a fantastic game and as North End tried tirelessly to unlock the Villa defence, the crowd began to rise to them and their all out effort.

A Spavin free kick was headed on by Heppolette but Ham failed to connect properly from a good position. They came close again when Heppolette had a tremendous shot from the edge of the area blocked by Brian Godfrey, the former North End player. The ball ran to Bird whose first time effort was blocked again by a packed Villa defence, resulting in a terrific scramble that Aitken eventually defused by shielding the ball back to Dunn.

Heppolette, Spavin and Wilson then combined well with Dunn finally grasping the ball from Wilson as he cut in from the right.

Villa then won two corners in quick succession which came to nothing, but then Kelly was called upon to make a brilliant diving save from Geoff Vowden, Villa's in form striker, after his fierce low drive.

Ham bolted down the left wing, then cut in at pace from the byline. He fired the ball in his stride and only a sliding stop in the mud by Turnbull kept North End goalless. Clark was then put clear by Spavin, but his left foot curling shot was saved at full stretch by the sprawling Dunn at the foot of the post.

All too soon the match was over. Both teams were covered in mud, hadn't scored a goal between them but had put on a pulsating display of football. The crowd applauded the 22 players off in appreciation of a fine display. A crowd of over 22,000 had spent their money well.

There had to be some bad news. It came in the form of the football results from my friends transistor radio as we squelched our way home..... Doncaster Rovers 0 Fulham 1 and Brighton 0 Halifax Town 2.

I had fully expected Halifax Town's run to have come to an end at Brighton, but on they went, as sharp as a surgeon's knife. Sadly for us, they were obviously the team with the strong finish. The top of the table read, Fulham with 58 points from 44 games, North End with 56 from 43, and Halifax with 54 from 43.

The playground split was still favouring a North End promotion as I recall, but I will admit to having cold feet about it. After all, we still had to visit Wrexham and Fulham - who were both very good teams - before completing the season with the re-arranged fixture against Rotherham United.

Before you could seemingly even reflect on the superb Saturday entertainment, North End were on duty again on the following Monday evening, away at Wrexham.

Lancashire Evening

Football Post

No. 26,182 APRIL 24, 1971. SATURDAY 3p

ALAN SPAVIN

Skem's dream comes true: Halifax and Fulham win

Howley steps in for PNE match

PNE IN GOAL-LESS THRILLER!

AFTER a tremendous marathon in the mud, Preston North End managed to gain a point in their thriller against Aston Villa at Deepdale.

Verdict on the big match

Cliffhanger as Preston go for goal

No bite

Great save

Swindon v Carlisle

Stoke v Man. C.

Scoreboard

DIVISION 1

DIVISION 2

RUGBY LEAGUE

RUGBY UNION

SCOTTISH DIV 1

DIVISION 3

DIVISION 4

AMATEUR CUP FINAL

Dagenham v Skem'le

Man. U. v Ipswich

SCOTTISH DIV 2

T.V. SOCCER

FOOTBALL FINAL SCORES

Do we need pro refs?—Pages 4 and 6

The Welshmen would be a worry for North End, standing just outside the promotion race. There was no good news coming out of Deepdale.

Ingram was still sidelined, and now Ham was a serious doubt. It all seemed that it was going a little pear shaped, as Ball announced he was tagging young Norman Lloyd on to the squad that climbed on the afternoon coach to North Wales.

Wrexham, as they say these days, 'went for it.' They played fast attacking football, which I have no doubt reflecting on this game approaching 50 years later, was a joy for their fans to behold - it sounded like that anyway from the noise they made. But it had got to the stage now where I selfishly just wanted North End to collapse over the promotion white line.

I didn't really care how they played; they had proved to me long before this game that they had played well enough this season to be fully deserving of some well earned success.

The knots in the pit of my stomach were tightened as it announced that Norman 'Norrie' Lloyd would replace Bobby Ham in the attack. What a task this was for the lad. Already 'Ingram-less,' North End's attack was being led by a very keen 21 year old, who had appeared just once for the first team earlier in the season.

He was to let nobody down! He had been thrust into the limelight towards the end of the previous season and asked to do a similar job as the good ship North End was sinking rapidly - duly returning five goals in just 13 appearances - so he wasn't a complete novice.

Life soon became almost unbearable though after around 20 minutes in, as Wrexham took the lead. Kelly had wonderfully saved a header from Ray Smith by pushing it around the post. Arfon Griffiths floated the corner into the penalty area and big Wrexham centre half Edwin May headed goalwards, the ball becoming loose in front of the North End goal line. Smith was there to poke the ball over the line, much to the joy of the home crowd.

It had been an end to end game before that; North End still going for a win despite their mini injury crisis. It continued in that way; Ball and Cox waving arms and bellowing instructions constantly.

And then...some good news at last! North End equalised through the one and only Norrie Lloyd!

Spavin fed a ball through, resulting in a chase between Lloyd and centre half May for control. May came second, and as Lloyd closed in on the keeper, he calmly slotted it past him into the empty net. He was mobbed by his team mates, as the Gentry and the rest of the North End fans present made themselves heard.

Reflecting about the game at half time, the way Wrexham were playing, a point gained here by North End would be a good result. It would deny Halifax Town a move into a promotion slot even if they won their away game at Torquay in midweek.

That obviously wasn't North End's intention as the second half kicked off - the excitement continued with both teams trying to nose in front. In defence, the new partnership of Hawkins and Bird showed their authority, breaking down many an attack, and rolling the ball back into Spavin's path. Ross and McNab, completing the back four, were also alert to any danger. Indeed, it was McNab who deflected away a powerfully hooked shot from Rob Park with a diving header, when a goal looked certain.

Lloyd very nearly replicated his first goal as the game drew to its close, running onto a Hawkins clearance which had sort of morphed into a through ball, but this time was foiled by Dave Gaskell, the home keeper.

So it was a point; and a very well earned one. It was another big hurdle out of the way. Just a case now of sitting back and seeing how Halifax and Fulham fared in their midweek games.

Post match, the managers had very differing views. John Neal, the Wrexham coach claimed that his team had taught Preston how to play.

"We are the side who should be going up," he claimed.

Ball meanwhile paid tribute to his battling team, whose form suggested they were flagging. *"My lads are giving me everything they have and I can't ask any more of them. We will fight until we drop of exhaustion."*

Tuning through the dials of the Radio on Wednesday evening trying to find up to date information on the Fulham and Halifax games was impossible. The late BBC television News started far too early at 9pm in those days to include final football scores and the Radio 2 Sports Desk was at 10:50, so it was a case of staying up for News at Ten, and wait for somebody like Reginald Bosanquet to deliver the news that I had waited an age to hear. "Torquay United 2 Halifax Town 0." Brilliant! They were human after all!

The above result was delivered after the Bradford City v Fulham game, where the visitors won 3-2, to make certain of promotion. Good luck to them too. They had virtually led the Third Division from the off, and it was well deserved. That all meant that we needed just 2 points from our last 2 games and that Saturday's away match at Craven Cottage would in effect be the championship decider.

Interestingly, messages of North End's impending doom were relayed in the LEP towards the end of the week. These weren't from opposition fans though; these were from the Fulham players and manager!

"Preston will not stop us winning the championship. They have no chance and we will win easily." - **Steve Earle**, Fulham centre forward

"I can't see us failing in front of our own fans in such an important game as this. We are promoted now and relaxed, and with the tension gone the lads should play even better. The champagne has been ordered. We will do a lap of honour before the game and have a few drinks after."
- **Bill Dodgin Jnr**, Fulham manager

Meanwhile back at Deepdale, Ball was being a little cautious. *"Obviously we will do our utmost to beat Fulham....but you can get a bit greedy."*

He reported that his players were full of confidence, and fully aware that their task at Fulham was their hardest of the season. Bobby Ham was likely to be fit and ready to play; Ball's quandary was the eventual formation and whether Wrexham hero Lloyd kept his place.

The result implications for the game at Craven Cottage were seemingly endless. Fulham, already promoted, needed just a draw to give them the title. For North End, a win would secure promotion, and a further win at home to Rotherham in their final match, would give them top spot. A draw or defeat for Preston left them exposed to Halifax Town coming up on the rails, although Halifax Town's winning margins would have to be large.

May

Fulham, Rotherham United, Champions of Division Three!

Saturday, May 1st 1971, 3pm. North End's entire season would hinge on their performance at Craven Cottage.

Wearing their away kit of red shirts, white shorts and white socks, Graham Hawkins led the team out from the corner of the stadium, to the cheers of the many North Enders who had made their way to the capital. BBC TV cameras were present, recording the clash for their 'Match of the Day' programme.

Bobby Ham was passed fit and led the North End attack with Norrie Lloyd keeping his place after his heroics at Wrexham in midweek.

Ball made his way down the touchline to the dugouts, with Arthur Cox, Harry Hubbick, substitute Dave Wilson and squad members George Lyall and David Hughes. His stride was brisk and purposeful, and hopefully the team talk he had just delivered had put the players in a similar frame of mind. According to Ricky Heppolette in a later interview, Ball kept repeating, *"Attack, attack, attack..."* as the players prepared themselves.

Handshakes were exchanged between the captains; Barry Lloyd of Fulham and our very own Graham Hawkins - the North End skipper looking a lot more confident than I felt!

The game kicked off in front of a crowd of approaching 26,000 and both teams tested the water with decent attacking moves. Fulham were roared on by the home fans whenever they made a forward movement. They thought they had gone close when neat play led to a cross with North End's goal exposed, but the linesman was stood bolt upright with his flag raised for offside to quell any North End fears.

North End punched back, and won a corner on the left, which was taken by the ever busy Clark. Curling it in to just around the six yard box, it was met firmly by the head of Hawkins and went inches over the bar.

The match began to flow, and it became obvious that a draw was not on the menu for either side. Spavin put Clark through but the defender was too quick for him, then Steve Earle set winger Les Barrett up nicely, but his progress was halted as the ball went for a corner. This in turn directly led to another as North End didn't clear their lines, but Kelly dealt with the resulting shot on goal without problem.

The North End defence was instilling some confidence into their followers at the ground, who were making quite a noise, letting the players know they weren't alone.

Ross overlapped well, and found Spark who flicked the ball on to Ham, who had his back to goal. He cheekily back heeled the ball and was unlucky in that Webster the Fulham keeper was in the right place to save. North End were starting to dominate, and to every travelling North End fan's sheer delight, took the lead on 22 minutes.

It was a move created by the Football Gods! Well noted for their invention under Ball from any dead ball situation, North End won a corner on the right, and the players assumed their set positions in the Fulham penalty area.

It went like this. Lloyd was hanging around the penalty spot, Ham at the near post, with Hawkins and Heppolette near the edge of the box close together. Lloyd then wandered back to Hawkins for a quick word, and then hastily resumed position.

Clark set the ball in the quadrant and looked up. Seeing this, Lloyd made his move, running toward Clark and dragging three Fulham defenders into a straight line behind him. Ham also moved forward dragging the defender off the near post.

At the same instant, Hawkins and Heppolette ran forward toward the freshly exposed space; Hawkins toward the centre of the goal and Heppolette to the left side.

Meanwhile, Clark took the corner and floated the ball accurately, Lloyd met it and using its pace flicked it backwards - the increased elevation beautifully lifting it over heads of the string of defenders trailing behind him, taking them instantly out of the game.

The ball was just too high for even Hawkins' magnificent leap in front of goal and passed over him, but a now-in-the-clear Heppolette, reached the falling ball with a diving header and buried it into the bottom left hand corner.

It was sheer class; and a goal worthy of such an occasion.

It was like stirring up a wasps nest. Fulham went on a sustained period of attack. It took a goal line clearance from Hawkins to keep out a Barrett centre, while Bird was very cool when he disarmed a posse of approaching home forwards single handedly.

North End eventually slowed down the pace of the game and reasserted themselves. Spavin unleashed a powerful shot which was well saved by Webster, then North End almost went two up after winning a corner on the left.

Clark centred, and Ham got his head to the ball which seemed to hang in the air as it went towards the far corner of the goal with Webster beaten. Unfortunately for Ham, a defender was stationed on the line and headed clear.

Earle made progress but a coming together with Spark ended with the

Fulham striker blatantly aiming a fierce kick at the defenders shin which left him on the ground. The referee spoke to both players, but gave Fulham the free kick for shirt pulling! Earle had come across to the North End fans as a 'big time Charlie' after his midweek predictions, and the North End fans let him know it.

North End saw off a late Fulham rally, backed by deafening encouragement from their fans before the whistle went for the break.

If that little spell by Fulham had seemed threatening, it was nothing compared to what was coming North End's way when the match resumed.

They were locked in their own half, desperately trying to shield their penalty area as the home side threw everything they had at them. Earle tried a shot which bravely Kelly smothered at the feet of the onrushing Johnston. The keeper cleared the ball but needed attention, eventually regaining his feet; the magical 'L'eau de Hubbick' once more revitalising an injured Northender.

Hawkins then intercepted a clever lob by Jimmy Conway, and Barrett, obviously told to cut in at pace from the wing, ballooned a shot over the bar.

North End were living of scraps at this point, breaking forward to relieve the pressure whenever possible. Ham nearly punished the home side when Webster fumbled a cross, just managing to regain the ball as the forward homed in on the chance.

Hawkins was having a magnificent game, and with Bird alongside him the pairing were surely the best in the division, if not beyond. Moving Spark into midfield had paid dividends too; his strength in winning many a 50/50 contest was there for all to see.

A penalty shout when Ham went down in the Fulham box was waved away by the ref, and Fulham immediately put North End under pressure. They got into a tangle at the back due to lack of numbers, but

Spark eventually took control making a decisive clearance.

McNab then headed away a dangerous cross and Spark once more broke up a dangerous move on the edge of the North End box.

North End had really been under the cosh, and the whole team had played well in repelling wave after wave of attacks. One thing was for certain – the team of a year previously would have been several goals behind at this stage.

The North End resilience was heartening their fans, who were now shouting just as loud as their opposites.

As the game entered its final phase, Fulham launched a last, all out offensive. Striker Vic Halom was brought on signaling their intent on getting the goal they needed for the title.

Indeed it was Halom after being put through on the right by Barrett who shot into the side netting with only Kelly to beat, straight after coming on. As he walked back down the pitch he passed North End left back McNab who summed up the feelings for all North Enders as he pumped both fists in celebration at the miss towards the away fans.

Barrett then crossed beautifully on the run from the left, and Halom's header went wide of the far post. Opportunities seemed to coming faster than ever for Fulham now, and it was panic stations again as a loose ball fell to Barrett on the left, his curling shot having beaten Kelly being cleared off the line by the energetic Heppolette.

There were desperate shouts from the North End dugout, fists being clenched and wide open palms being raised to indicate there were five remaining minutes. The tension was unbearable, but Clark earned applause from the dugout by using up some precious seconds on the left.

Fulham weren't finished yet, as what I humbly consider the 'defining 'play' of North End's and indeed, Fulham's season unfolded.

North End cleared a ball towards the centre circle but it was instantly volleyed to Barrett on the left, catching North End's forward surging defence on their heels somewhat.

This left Barrett in the clear homing in from the left, as the returning Hawkins tried to force him towards the byline. It was too late; Barrett drilled in a perfect low cross that was passing Kelly, stood alone at the near post.

Kelly was stranded; frozen in time, looking directly at Halom who was speeding in to meet the ball five yards out. Nobody else was in sight. At that instant, the championship and maybe even promotion dream was all over.

As Halom's foot was literally poised to connect, a red blur executed what must be the best goal saving slide tackle in football history.

The red blur was John Bird.

As if conjured up by an illusionist to appear under Halom's feet, Bird stopped the ball dead - and cleanly - with such aplomb that the striker's upper body motion continued while his feet stayed still against the ball. While Halom ended up hugging the goal post, Kelly thankfully just flopped on the prostrate Bird and the loose ball. Un-be-lieve-able!

Time was virtually up when McNab hoofed a clearance half way up the stand. One last long throw came in from Conway. This was cleared but the ball was fed back down the right wing and crossed quickly, reaching Horne at the far side in the clear. Steadying himself, he curled a great shot in, but it went inches over the bar.

The goal kick was taken, and then Mr. Gow blew the final whistle. What a sight to behold! Many North End fans invaded the pitch, so did Ball, who kissed the turf; the rest of the party hugging the players who had done the club so proud.

A truly wonderful day in North End's history!

Lancashire Evening

Football Post

No. 26,186 SATURDAY, MAY 1st, 1971. 3p

APRIL CASH SALE

FREE-STAY HOLIDAY

GEORGE SEYMOUR

CONGRATULATIONS!

Preston can be proud again

Certainly, the fans can be proud again!

PNE PROMOTED – THANKS TO HEPPY!

THEY'RE UP! Preston North End shook the Metropolis with a capital performance at Craven Cottage this afternoon to beat Fulham 1-0 to clinch promotion back to the Second Division at the first attempt!

Not so swinging

North End Verdict

Fulham squander late chances

Nerves

World record

Salver

Friendly

GOING UP!

Scoreboard

DIVISION 1

DIVISION 2

DIVISION 3

DIVISION 4

RUGBY LEAGUE

PREMIER LGE.

SCOTTISH DIV 1

SOUTHERN LGE.

F.A. CHALLENGE TROPHY

Crystal P. v Everton

Wolves v Burnley

Carlisle v Sheff. W.

Peterboro' v Barrow

Kelly gets Eire call up

T.V. SOCCER

FOOTBALL FINAL SCORES

For the rest of the weekend I was in dreamland. I saved the *Football Post* of course, as you can see. Would there ever be a week like this again?! But there wasn't much time to dwell on heroics – we had the title to win on Tuesday night against Rotherham United at Deepdale.

There was time, however to take in what a certain impartial spectator thought of the game at Craven Cottage. This just happened to be Sir Alf Ramsey, who had taken the opportunity to view the crucial proceedings.

"It was a pity that one side had to lose, but it was a fine match. Certainly in terms of football skill there was plenty of good play, and Preston's Alan Spavin was outstanding."

He couldn't help but comment on John Bird's performance too. *"Did Preston really buy him for only £5,000 from Doncaster Rovers?"* he asked the reporters. *"Amazing."*

Under the headline "**NOW THE CHAMPIONSHIP ?**" Monday's LEP sports page captured the moment of North End's fine goal.

Ricky Heppolette has the privilege of scoring the goal that takes North End back into the Second Division

Alan Spavin was happy too. Rumoured to have won the Third Division Player of the Year Trophy, he explained that the team were determined to gain two points after reading the comments coming out of Craven Cottage during the week.

"We showed them, didn't we? We turned it on in the first half and our defence was magnificent in the second."

Dashing home from school on Tuesday, with homework to do - thank you teachers, one and all - I also wanted my tea early as the school was full of talk that there would be a massive crowd at Deepdale and maybe some would be locked out.

The LEP reported that North End would be unchanged after the Fulham victory, with Ball saying that they would do everything in their power to make this a night to remember.

Scramming my tea down, after taking great care over my homework - not - I left for Deepdale at just after 6pm.

My Dad thought I had lost my marbles, but hey ho; I knew what I was doing!

By the time I got to the ground the queues were forming like long tentacles and just opting to get from Lowthorpe Road to the West Paddock via the ginnel behind the Town End was a terrible choice. I eventually made it though and was in position by around 6:45pm.

The excitement and expectation was easy to sense and feel as the crowd reached massive proportions, with finally 28,224 assembled to see North End not only ascend, but hopefully to ascend with the Third Division title...

It was Rotherham United, including a 20 year old Roy Tunks who poked their noses out of the tunnel first, to line up ready to applaud North End onto the pitch. The noise was deafening as the Lilywhites ran through the Rotherham 'corridor' and onto the pitch; this was something else I had never witnessed a North End team enjoy.

There was something different about the team too, they just looked confident; something that had been a little lacking through the recent weeks.

Promoted North End run through the corridor of Rotherham Utd players before the kick off

After some early sparring, North End started to get to grips with the task in hand. Just before the half hour mark, some neat interplay between Clark, Heppolette and Spark saw Spavin teed up for a shot on goal. He made no mistake, the effort swirling high into the top right hand corner of the Town End net, way beyond goalkeeper Roy Tunks' reach.

The noise was terrific, and my pals and I hardly stopped talking about it all, when North End doubled their lead – and how!

At various times during the season they had pulled out the 'Falling Wall' free kick blueprint out of their manual, each time getting closer to actually scoring from it. Their best execution of it to date was a month previously at Bristol Rovers, where only a finger tip save by the Rovers keeper saved the day.

North End had been awarded a free kick near the Rotherham box on the West Paddock side. Spavin stood over the ball and four North End players – I seem to recall Ham and Lloyd being two of them – stood in front of the Rotherham wall. Everyone in the crowd knew what was coming, and sure enough as Spavin was about to shoot the ball, the four Northenders broke in all directions.

The ball soon flew over both sets of players, curling high toward that top right hand corner again. Tunks dived and almost got there, but the ball hit the back of the net to another deafening appreciation from the crowd of some fine North End play.

To say that Spavin was ever so slightly delighted was the under-statement of the year! He was leaping about everywhere at his handiwork; and what better stage for it to come off for the first time...

Indeed that confidence was now brimming, as Lloyd, Heppolette and Hawkins were all unlucky with good efforts on goal.

While all this was going on, the home crowd was chanting either for Ball or the team at a very noisy level.

The second half continued as though half time hadn't happened, with complete Preston domination.

Further reward was eventually reaped when Clark fired in an inswinging corner, several players from each team attempting to head it, all of whom missed. The ball was eventually hooked away from under the bar by a Rotherham defender.

While all that was happening the linesman was already signaling to the ref that the ball actually had made it over the line, so Clark was credited with his fourth goal of the season. Further joy all round.

This was the cue for some of the more 'over enthusiastic' supporters to invade the pitch, causing a couple of minutes delay.

Finally, it was all over, and then there really was a pitch invasion – of biblical proportions. Me? Well, I admit to climbing over the perimeter fence to walk onto the pitch, but it never really got further than that, as it now appeared that the 28,000 crowd had transferred from the stands to the turf and got there before me.

I did see a back view of Graham Hawkins being chaired off, and the players appearing in the Pavilion Stand where they threw their shirts down to the fans.

The whole vicinity of the ground was rocking with football chants, "We are the Champions," "Preston, Preston..."

18 EVENING POST, WEDNESDAY, MAY 5, 1971

Massive Deepdale crowd salutes North End

Ball's boys clinch title

● We are the champions . . . and it's a champagne celebration in the dressing room for George Ross, Gerry Ingram and Jim McNab.

● JUBILATION—thousands of fans on the pitch after the match.

We are the champions!

THAT THIRD DIVISION Championship Trophy will be presented to Preston North End at a special reception on the balcony of the Harris Art Gallery next Monday.

This is the physical, tangible reward which Preston will receive for gaining promotion back to the Second Division at the first attempt in the best possible way.

By Norman Shakeshaft

● Hero of the night, two-goal Alan Spavin prefers to wait for his champagne. His first after-match drink was a quiet cuppa. The bubbly bottles still stand unopened.

● A champagne shower for team captain Graham Hawkins from manager Alan Ball. Delighted club chairman Tom Nicholson is on the right.

Pictures by ROY PAYNE

Great Times!

In just short 12 months, the massive shortcomings at Deepdale had been addressed, by an energetic new manager, the very same players (bar just a couple), his coaching staff and, it has to be said, a supportive board of directors. All deserved congratulation as their synergies had put North End back into Division Two with a more than welcome momentum behind them.

TWO GOLDEN GOALS

● GOAL ONE—Alan Spavin's first goal in the match against Rotherham last night. Tunks had no chance, as this shot swirls into the top corner.

● GOAL TWO.—Spavin's second, this time a gem direct from a free kick. The unsighted Tunks can only make a vain attempt to save.

How the Evening Post displayed Alan Spavin's two goal salvo against Rotherham United

The playing squad deserved much praise; such was the impact of their great season. A week or so later, a salute to this North End team was held on the square in front of the Harris Library. A large crowd saw the team individually introduced on the balcony and hold the Championship Trophy aloft whilst receiving congratulations from both civic and football dignitaries alike.

At that moment, for a football mad 14 year old stood near the front of that crowd, who had previously only ever witnessed doom, gloom and problems in respect of his home town team, it certainly didn't get any better than this!

To top the season off completely, Alan Spavin was deservedly named as Division Three Player of the Year.

The LEP even issued a special edition of that evening's newspaper...

Lancashire
Evening Post

TUESDAY, MAY 11th, 1971. 3p

Salute to the Champions

Picture by JACK CATLOW

5,000 say: Well done, PNE

WE ARE THE CHAMPIONS

TRIUMPH

Pictures: NORMAN WIGGINS

The Squad

Rather than give the standard 'Official Programme' background 'Pen Pictures' for each player, here is my take on the 1970/71 Preston North End squad.

Goalkeeper – Alan Kelly

Alan Kelly always looked the Eire international goalkeeper he was. He delivered simplicity, safety, the spectacular and great awareness. Quite simply there was no other keeper in the division who compared. An ever present in 1970/71, with 19 league clean sheets. A little later in his North End career, Brian Moore the ITV commentator observed during a televised game that Kelly was, "more than worthy of higher status than Division Two," which sort of says it all....

Full Back – George Ross

I can find words that would justifiably pay homage to George Ross all day, but the best compliment I can say is that if his name was missing from the team sheet, then North End just didn't look right. He was a cornerstone of the team. Uncomplicated but skilled player with great defensive qualities and a superb turn of speed when overlapping down the right under the Ball system. A most loyal and reliable team member.

Full Back – Jim McNab

Jim McNab must have wished he could have forgotten his first two seasons at Deepdale. Under Ball, he gained a new lease of life and became one of the division's outstanding full backs. Like Ross, he enjoyed the overlap and often turned up to assist the attack – his goal against Fulham at Deepdale I will never forget.

Full Back – John McMahon

Willing, enthusiastic and powerful, John McMahon was thrust into the first team as cover for the injured full backs but demonstrated his versatility by eventually covering three positions. Never let the side down, and would become a North End stalwart in years to come.

Centre Back / Midfield – Alex Spark

At home whether playing alongside Hawkins in defence or Spavin in midfield, Alex Spark always gave his all. He had a monster tackle technique, a hard and accurate shot and nothing was ever a lost cause. The sort of utility man any team with aspirations needs.

Centre Back & Captain – Graham Hawkins

It must have been easy for Ball to nominate Graham Hawkins as captain. He had it all. Blessed with commanding presence and a reading of the game that isn't conferred on many, he led by example throughout the season. Never taking a backward step, he organised and protected. Not short of all round ability either, often supplementing the attack with his aerial skills. Ever present. Colossus.

Centre Back – John Bird

The record shows that John Bird only played seven first team games at the very end of the season. However, in each and every game he demonstrated his class; exceptional in both tackle and distribution. No example better than that miracle promotion saving, sliding tackle near the end of the game at Craven Cottage. Not many players are coveted enough to prompt managerial resignations, but Bird unwittingly was a few years later.

Midfield – Alan Spavin

Club Player of the Year, Division Three Player of the Year, lauded by opposition managers alike and best of all, Sir Alf Ramsey. Seemed to revel in heavy, unfavourable conditions when others didn't want to know. Imperious passer of the ball, with vision far above Division Three level. Wasn't in the first flush of youth in 1970/71, so made the ball do the running for him. Absolutely pivotal to the teams' prospects of success. Spectacularly loyal; the ultimate club man.

Midfield – Ricky Heppolette

Provided youth, support, creativity and the added element of how to finish a move off with devastating effect. His performances made him a sought after player for bigger clubs during the season. Possessed a wonderful 'engine', and later in his career played under the tutelage of Terry Venables. He contributed eight vital goals during 70/71, none more so than the one that secured promotion at Craven Cottage.

Midfield – George Lyall

Skilled, industrious, hard tackling with the added value of a hammer shot, Lyall played alongside Spavin and Heppolette to great effect. His never say die attitude fitted into the Ball style of play like a glove, amply demonstrated in the Torquay home game, where his efforts alone in driving the team on almost turned a two goal deficit into a win.

Forward – Bobby Ham

Ball's desire to get Bobby Ham onto the pitch in a North End shirt went back to the first few weeks of the season. After a string of hurdles were finally overcome, Ham arrived...and delivered and delivered and delivered. With a playing style in the mould of a Greaves or a Lineker, his main domain was the penalty area, rooting out and grazing on any half chances. As well as occasionally turning provider, his return of 11 goals from 29 League games proved to one and all that he certainly knew where the 'onion bag' was.

Forward – Gerry Ingram

The transformation in Gerry Ingram's fortunes during 70/71 was startling. Under Ball, North End were tactically much more aware and the flanks were used to provide Ingram with ammunition to constantly fire at the opposition goal, and the big striker didn't disappoint. His confidence returned in abundance, banging in 22 League goals in 39 appearances. A massive contribution.

Forward – Clive Clark

Missing the first part of the season due to injury, he re-established himself and made the left wing position his own. A player with real pedigree, having played in Wembley Finals for West Brom, his playing style was one of speed, skill and wholehearted endeavour. Riling the opposition fans with the odd swallow dive seemed to spur him on even more. Must have been Ingram's best friend, as he provided countless opportunities for the big centre forward.

Forward – David Wilson

Dave Wilson always gave me the impression there was even more in his locker than we sometimes saw. Don't get me wrong - he was always a favourite of mine; he often left full backs on their backsides or stumbling in his wake as he glided past them demonstrating wing play at its best. He wasn't averse to bagging the odd goal either. Although an earlier move to Shankly's Liverpool didn't work out, he had already attained England U23 level by then...which would go some way to explain the fraught look on the face of many a full back.

Forward – David Hughes

Young, energetic and gave his all. His turn of pace was sometimes devastating; his crossing ability a delight. Overcame moronic treatment from spectators during a home Central League game to ram their comments down their throats with some great performances. Ball handled the situation well, and it was good to see this valued player always around the first team even when not selected.

Forward – Norman Lloyd

When it's announced that your leading scorer is ruled out for the crucial season run- in, as a fan you just hold your breath when a rookie is called in. But Ball knew what 'Norrie' was capable of and thrust him forward. He didn't disappoint. A crucial equaliser at Wrexham; an essential part of that North End set play at Fulham that yielded the winner and a more than competent role in the promotion party that was the Rotherham game were just desserts for his efforts. He also pulled a decent pint in later years....along with George Ross.

Forward – Willie Irvine

Willie Irvine was special. He signed on for North End in 1968 with what can only be described as a super human First Division (Premier League) record of 97 goals in 144 appearances for Burnley. In his book *'Together Again'* he reveals that he had never really recovered from a horrific injury sustained against Everton by the time he arrived at Deepdale. He then took another massive blow from David Webb of Chelsea in a FA Cup tie at Deepdale to a knee that resulted in ligament damage. That apart, he still managed to put 27 goals away for North End in only 81 outings. If he had enjoyed better service in his early days at North End, he would have been a scoring legend at Deepdale too. Willie never gave less than 100% and was as honest a player as you could get, and still held in high regard by those who saw him play. His record at both domestic and International level is there for all to see.

Forward – Frank Lee

Frank Lee was a very dependable player who appeared in just seven games for North End in 1970/71. Used exclusively as a winger by previous managers in the 60's, Lee was surprisingly given a roving midfield role by Ball at Shrewsbury and blew everyone away with his performance. He then fell ill, missed the next game, and never really got a toe hold back in the team. He was later transferred to Southport.

Midfield – Archie Gemmill

I think I'm right in saying that everybody who witnessed Archie play for North End followed his later, great career with a sense of pride. He was one of us. A top class midfielder with a superb engine, he eventually reached and took international football in his stride – who will ever forget that World Cup goal in Argentina against Holland or the full length of the field run to score for Forest against Arsenal? He only tied his bootlaces seven times for North End in 1970/71, before the inevitable pastures new beckoned. An all time great.

Manager – Alan Ball Snr

I mused at the start of this story that North End were starting off the season with the same squad of players that had performed so poorly the season before. How was it ever going to improve?

Well it did.

Put quite simply, besides one or two signings, the only major change was the manager.

He knew how to teach, encourage, invent, motivate, win football matches and as a result, turn around a football club on its knees.

What he did with the situation he was handed at Preston North End was quite remarkable, with some diehards since then even going as far as to describe Ball, Cox and Hubbick as the *'Three Wise Men from the East'*!

It has to be said, for those regular North End cash investors – the fans on the terrace – Alan Ball Senior was absolutely the right man at the right time.

Front Row — Left to right : George Lyall, Dave Wilson, Clive Clark, Alan Spavin, A. Ball (Manager), Bobby Ham, Bert Patrick, Ricky Heppolette, Alec Spark,
Standing — Left to right : A. Cox (Coach), George Ross, David Hughes, Gerry Ingram, Gerry Stewart, Alan Kelly, Jim McNab, John Bird, Graham Hawkins. H. Hubbick (Trainer).

APPEARANCES 1970-71

Football League Division III — P46, W22, D17, L7, Goals F63, A39—Pts. 61. Pos. 1

F.A. Cup	Lge. Cup		G (1)	RB (2)	LB (3)	RH (4)	CH (5)	LH (6)	OR (7)	IR (8)	CF (9)	IL (10)	OL (11)	Total
2	3	Alan KELLY	46	—	—	—	—	—	—	—	—	—	—	46
1	3	George ROSS........	—	43	—	—	—	—	—	—	—	—	—	43
1		Bert PATRICK	—	—	—	—	—	—	—	—	—	—	—	0
1	2	Jim McNAB	—	—	39	—	—	—	—	—	—	—	—	39
1	1	John McMAHON	—	3	7	1	—	—	—	—	—	—	—	11
2	3	Alec SPARK	—	—	—	38	—	—	—	—	—	4	—	42
		John BIRD	—	—	—	7	—	—	—	—	—	—	—	7
2	3	Graham HAWKINS ..	—	—	—	—	46	—	—	—	—	—	—	46
2	3	Richard HEPPOLETTE	—	—	—	—	—	6	18	5	—	9	—	38
1	3	David WILSON	—	—	—	—	—	—	19	2	—	—	—	21
	1	George LYALL	—	—	—	—	—	—	1	1	—	25	—	27
	3	Willie IRVINE........	—	—	—	—	—	—	—	3	3	7	—	13
		Norman LLOYD	—	—	—	—	—	—	—	1	3	—	—	4
	2	Archie GEMMILL	*(transferred)*			—	—	—	—	6	—	1	—	7
2		Bobby HAM	—	—	—	—	—	—	4	25	1	—	—	30
1	2	David HUGHES	—	—	—	—	—	—	4	—	—	—	9	13
2		Clive CLARK	—	—	—	—	—	—	—	—	—	—	32	32
2	2	Gerry INGRAM	—	—	—	—	—	—	—	—	39	—	—	39
2	2	Alan SPAVIN........	—	—	—	—	—	40	—	1	—	—	—	41
	1	Frank LEE	*(transferred)*			—	—	—	—	2	—	—	5	7
		Total	46	46	46	46	46	46	46	46	46	46	46	506

League Division III scorers — Ingram 22, Ham 11, Heppolette 8, Lyall 5, Spavin 4, Clark 4, Wilson 3, Irvine 1, Spark 1, McNab 1, Lloyd 1, Opponents 2 — Total 63

League Cup scorers (4)—Ingram 2, Irvine 1, Spavin 1. **F.A. Cup (1) Heppolette 1**

DIVISION THREE 1970-71

Final Table

	P.	W.	D.	L.	Goals F.	Goals A.	Pts.
Preston North End .	**46**	**22**	**17**	**7**	**63**	**39**	**61**
Fulham	46	24	12	10	68	41	60
Halifax Town	46	22	12	12	74	55	56
Aston Villa	46	19	15	12	54	46	53
Chesterfield..........	46	17	17	12	66	38	51
Bristol Rovers	46	19	13	14	69	50	51
Mansfield Town	46	18	15	13	64	62	51
Rotherham United ...	46	17	16	13	64	60	50
Wrexham	46	18	13	15	72	65	49
Torquay United	46	19	11	16	54	57	49
Swansea	46	15	16	15	59	56	46
Barnsley	46	17	11	18	49	52	45
Shrewsbury Town ...	46	16	13	17	58	62	45
Brighton	46	14	16	16	50	47	44
Plymouth Argyle	46	12	19	15	63	63	43
Rochdale	46	14	15	17	61	68	43
Port Vale	46	15	12	19	52	59	42
Tranmere Rovers	46	10	22	14	45	55	42
Bradford City	46	13	14	19	49	62	40
Walsall	46	14	11	21	51	57	39
Reading	46	14	11	21	48	85	39
Bury	46	12	13	21	52	60	37
Doncaster Rovers	46	13	9	24	45	66	35
Gillingham	46	10	13	23	42	67	33

CENTRAL LEAGUE 1970-71

Championship Table

	P.	W.	D.	L.	Goals F.	Goals A.	Pts.
Liverpool	42	30	6	6	82	29	66
Derby County	42	23	12	7	71	45	58
Everton	42	22	12	8	69	41	56
Manchester United ...	42	18	15	9	67	42	51
Burnley	42	18	15	9	77	61	51
Wolverhampton W....	42	16	13	13	68	54	45
Blackpool	42	17	11	14	60	55	45
Coventry City	42	14	16	12	69	50	44
Bolton Wanderers ...	42	16	12	14	73	71	44
West Bromwich Alb. .	42	15	13	14	65	59	43
Newcastle United	42	12	17	13	45	43	41
Sheffield United	42	15	11	16	64	64	41
Sheffield Wednesday	42	12	16	14	45	60	40
Huddersfield Town ..	42	14	11	17	71	72	39
Leeds United.........	42	11	17	14	52	56	39
Manchester City	42	16	6	20	61	83	38
Nottingham Forest ...	42	9	16	17	53	65	34
Stoke City	42	10	14	18	52	64	34
Bury	42	11	9	22	50	75	31
Preston North End .	42	11	8	23	53	90	30
Blackburn Rovers	42	11	6	25	47	84	28
Aston Villa	42	6	14	22	34	65	26

Preston North End Results 1970/71

1970	Rslt.	Pts	Atts.
Aug. 15—Halifax Town ....h	1–1	1	9646
,, **19—L.C.1 Stockport ....a**	**1–0**	**–**	**4353**
,, 22—Torquay United ....a	1–3	0	5908
,, 29—Bristol Rovers...............h	3–2	2	7957
,, 31—Wrexham ....h	3–2	2	10653
Sept. 5—Port Vale ....a	0–1	0	6954
,, **9—L.C.2 Torquay United ......a**	**3–1**	**–**	**6339**
,, 12—Reading ....h	4–1	2	9357
,, 19—Aston Villa ....a	0–2	0	26139
,, 22—Bury ....a	1–0	2	5821
,, 26—Fulham ....h	1–1	1	12103
,, 30—Shrewsbury Town............a	1–0	2	8026
Oct. 3—Bradford City ....a	2–0	2	7259
,, **6—L.C.3 West Brom ....h**	**0–1**	**–**	**18222**
,, 10—Mansfield Town..............h	2–1	2	12452
,, 17—Halifax Town ....a	0–1	0	5922
,, 19—Swansea City ....h	1–1	1	10328
,, 24—Plymouth Argyle ....a	1–1	1	9628
,, 31—Brighton & Hove Albion ....h	1–1	1	12567
Nov. 6—Doncaster Rovers (Friday) ....a	1–1	1	5300
,, 9—Barnsley ....h	3–1	2	11053
,, 14—Rochdale ....h	3–1	2	13460
,, **21—(F.A. Cup 1) Chester........h**	**1–1**	**–**	**15023**
,, **25— ,, ,, Replay ....a**	**0–1**	**–**	**11164**
,, 28—Chesterfield ....a	0–0	1	9720
Dec. 5—Gillingham ....h	1–0	2	10274
,, 19—Torquay United ....h	2–2	1	11637
,, 26—Tranmere Rovers ....a	3–3	1	7130
1971			
Jan. 9—Shrewsbury Town............h	2–0	2	11961
,, 15—Swansea City ....a	2–2	1	12776
,, 27—Walsall ....a	1–0	2	6435
,, 30—Chesterfield ....h	1–0	2	14020
Feb. 6—Gillingham ....a	1–2	0	4798
,, 13—Walsall ....h	1–0	2	11540
,, 20—Barnsley ....a	1–0	2	6619
,, 27—Brighton & Hove A. ....a	0–0	1	9957
Mar. 6—Plymouth Argyle ....h	1–0	2	12621
,, 8—Bury ....h	2–0	2	17136
,, 13—Rochdale ....a	2–1	2	10249
,, 16—Rotherham United............a	1–1	1	8291
,, 20—Doncaster Rovers ....h	4–0	2	14613
,, 27—Port Vale ....h	1–0	2	16591
April 3—Bristol Rovers...............a	0–0	1	10102
,, 10—Tranmere Rovers ....h	1–1	1	17382
,, 12—Reading........................a	0–1	0	7821
,, 13—Bradford City ....h	1–1	1	18694
,, 17—Mansfield Town ....a	1–3	0	7185
,, 24—Aston Villa ....h	0–0	1	22616
,, 26—Wrexham ....a	1–1	1	9662
May 1—Fulham ....a	1–0	2	25774
,, 4—Rotherham United............h	3-0	2	28224
,, **8—F.A. Cup Final**			

FRIENDLIES

Dec. 12—Grimsby Town	a	3–2	–
Feb. 8—Olympic XI	h	0–0	–
Mar. 2—Randers Freja (Denmark) ..	h	6–0	–

Bits and Pieces 1970/71

Saturday
December 5th
1970

Kick Off 3.00pm

North End

versus

Gillingham

A North End/Corporation Bus window poster printed in blue on a white background, that was usually pasted into place a week or so before the game. None would ever survive that long, disappearing faster than a bus conductor could issue a 2p ticket to town!

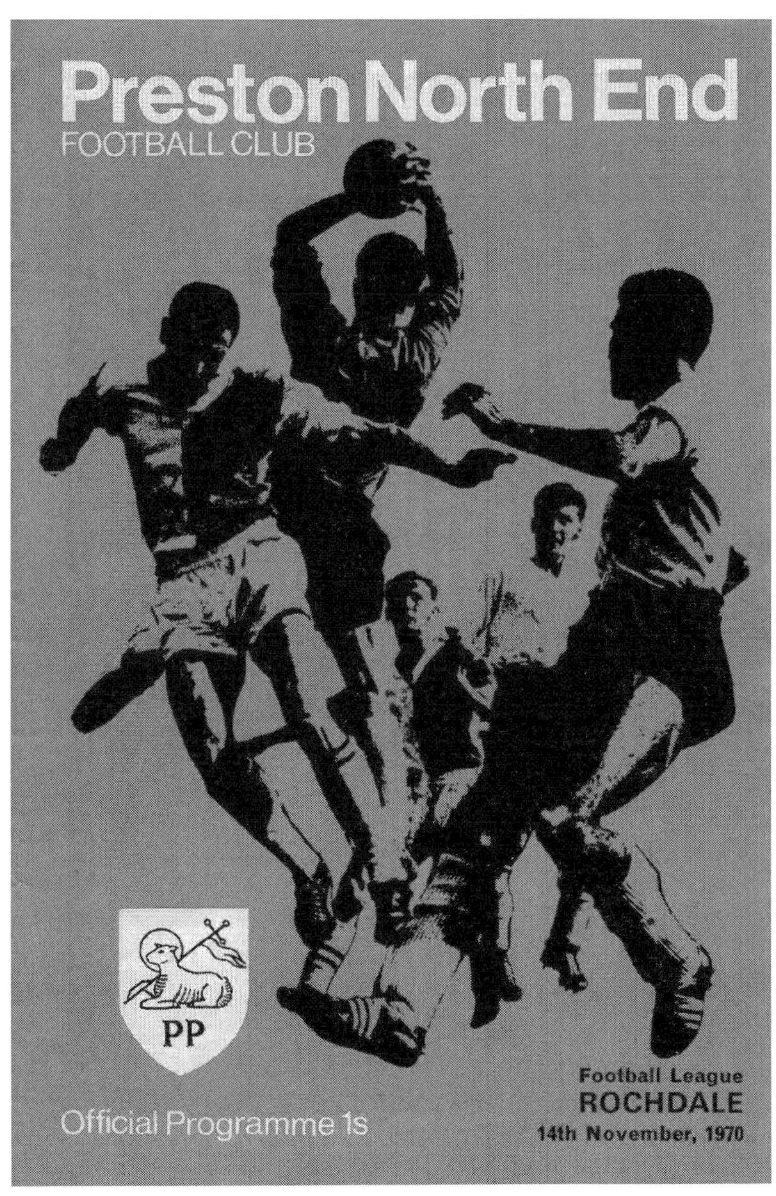

The iconic Preston North End Official Programme cover for 1970/71

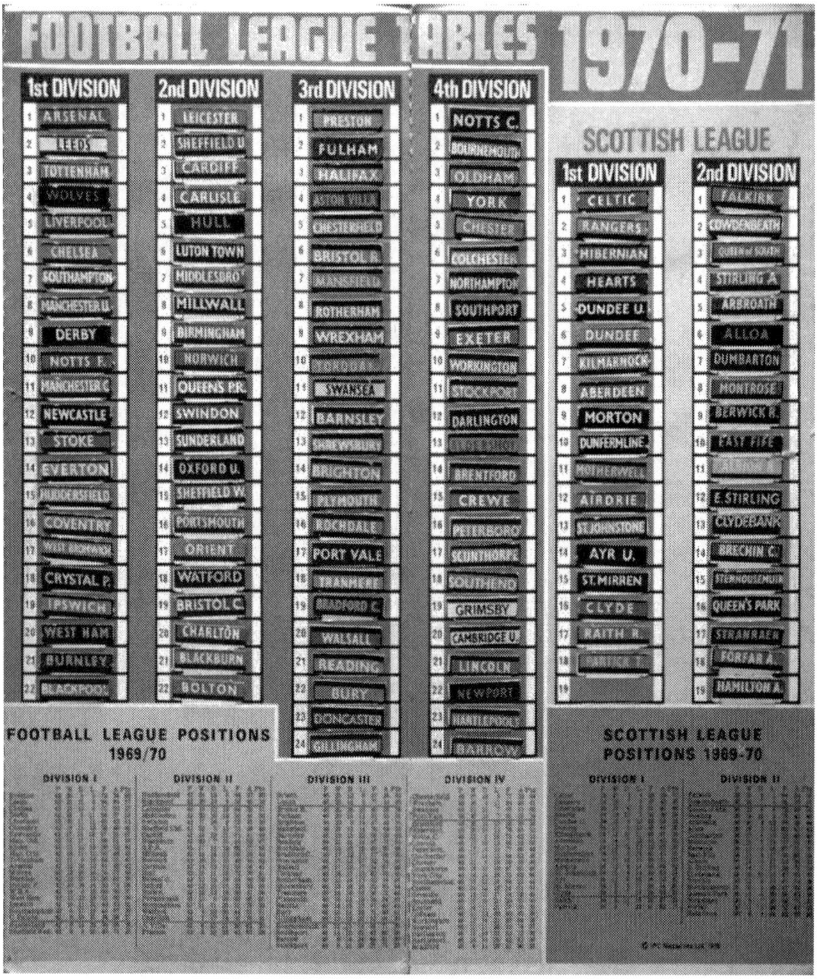

The infamous 'League Ladders'. Kids in the 70's didn't need computer games when they had these to fiddle with - literally! Each tab was in the team colours; these and the ladder were given away free in comics and football magazines in the weeks just before the season started.

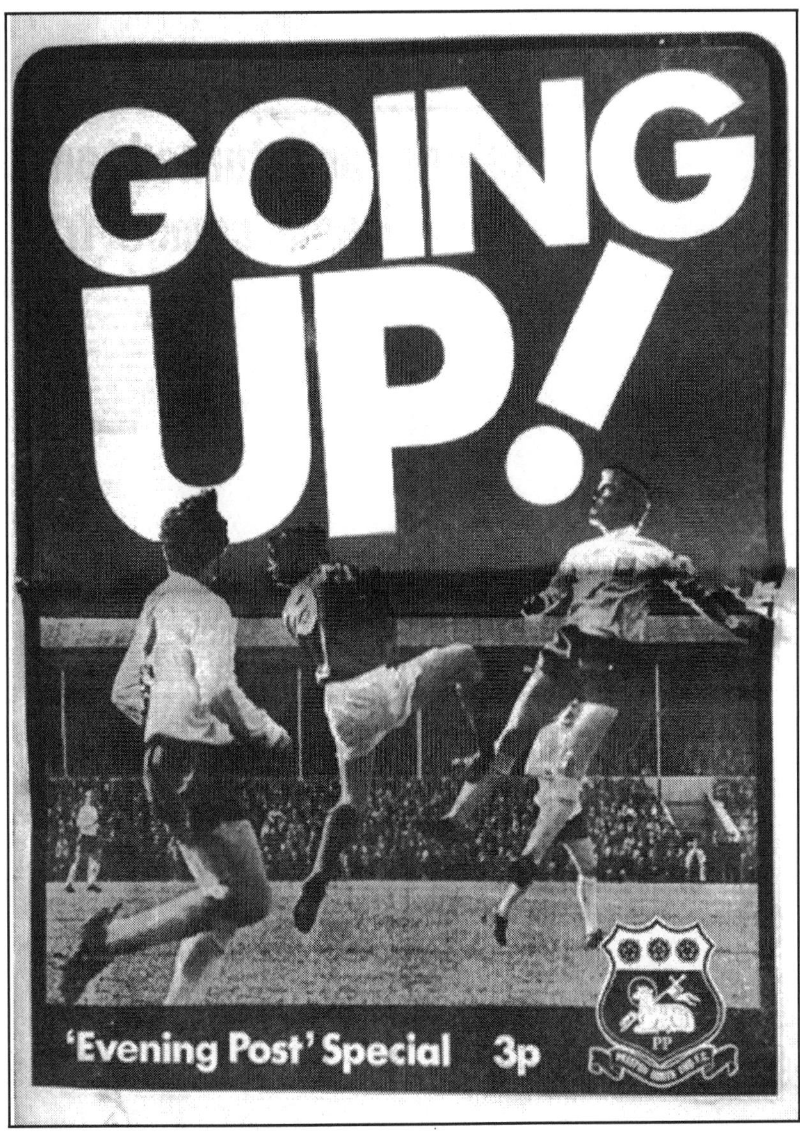

An Evening Post Special – 'Going Up!' was launched and on sale in time for the last home game of the season against Rotherham United. Full of pictures and words about the players, it celebrated North End's one season turnaround.

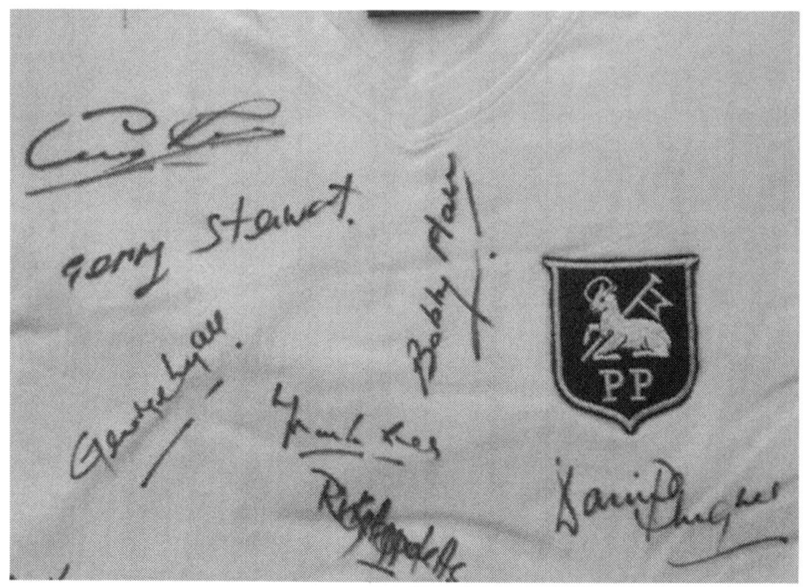

A few autographs of the 1970/71 team

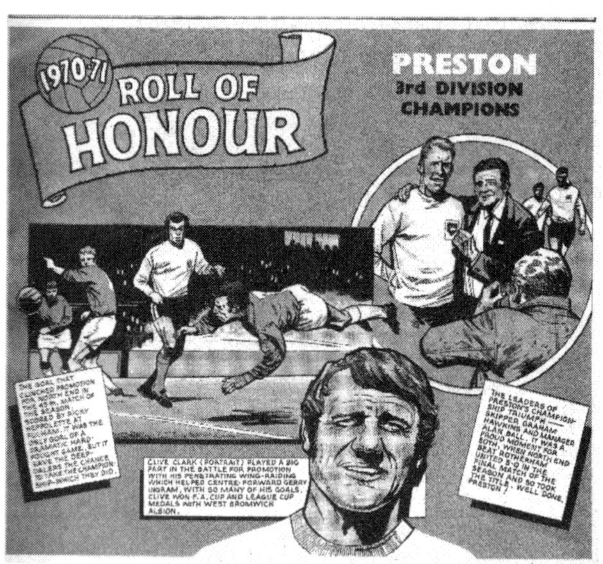

North End's exploits were news everywhere...........even in comics!

A Happy Christmas to one and all from Preston North End in 1970.

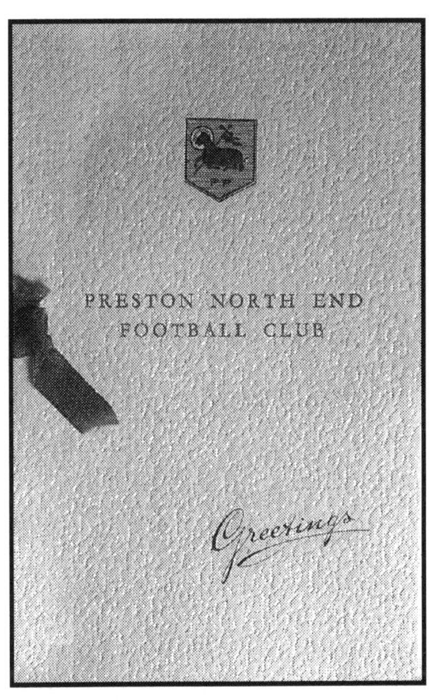

Unfortunately this rather lavishly embossed card, bedecked with blue ribbon and Preston crest wasn't sent out to the average fan...

...but I am sure the message conveying 'Hearty Greetings' inside was appreciated by the dignitaries who did receive one!

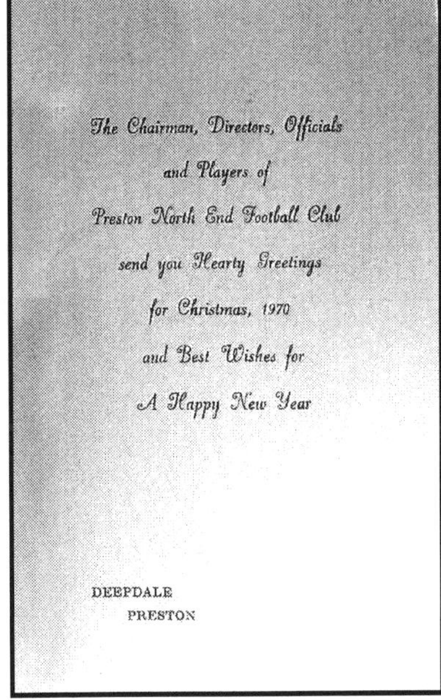

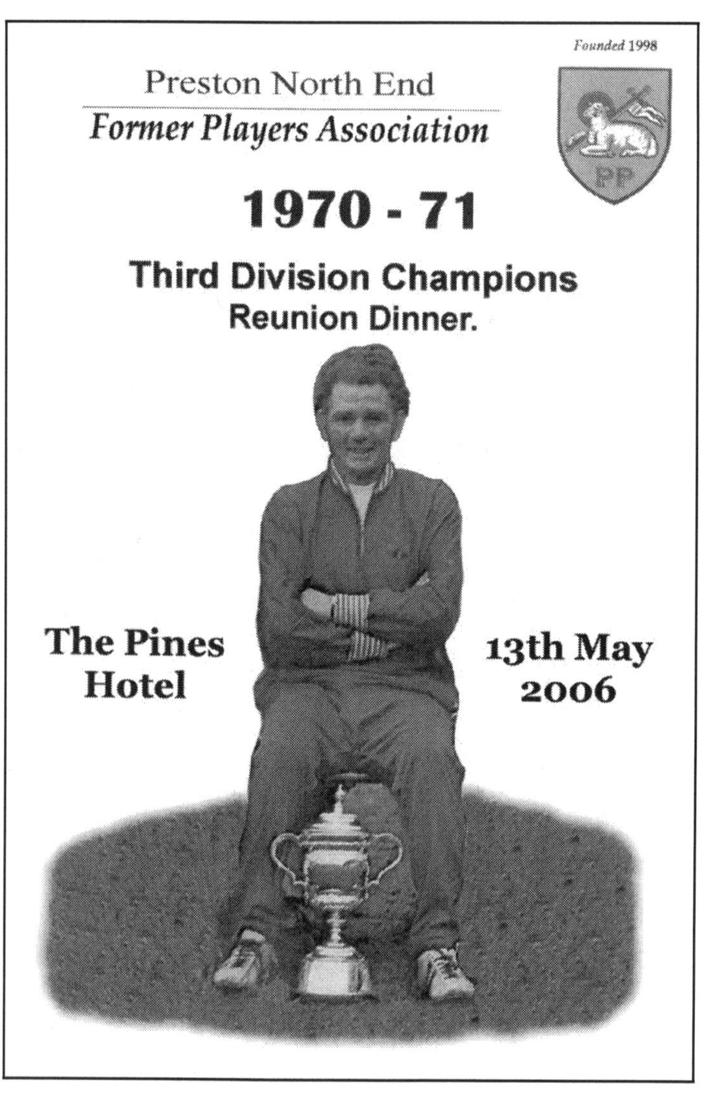

Souvenir marking the occasion of the Third Division Champions Reunion Dinner in 2006, organized by the PNE Former Players Association

Graham Hawkins

With the book just about finished, I decided I needed a Foreword to make it complete.

After plucking up enough courage, I contacted Graham Hawkins and ran the idea past him.

This eventually resulted in a get together that lasted some three hours, where he shared with me, not only his special memories of that North End season of 1970/71, but of his whole life in football. He has done an awful lot in the game.

It was bliss. The stories were just wonderful, as was his company that day.

What does come shining through about Graham though is his modesty.

I'm not quite sure if he believed me when I said I always mentally compare any subsequent North End defence with that of 1970/71, and always find myself leaning towards the one he led so admirably back then.

I had already written in my squad biography notes that I regard him as a 'colossus' of that North End team.

However, I would now like to add he is a 'colossus' of a gentleman too!

The May 4th Mantra*

(Sung repeatedly by the fans during the final game of the season v. Rotherham United)

In '69 when we went down into Division Three,
The Blackpool fans they cried out loud,
"That's the end of PNE."

Alan Ball he came,
We played the game,
We went to Fulham too,
We won one-nil and now we're back,
in Division Two.

We'll win the cup,
We'll win the league,
We'll go to Europe too,
And when we win the league this year,
We'll sing this song to you...

****there are variations!***

54448198R00102

Made in the USA
Charleston, SC
03 April 2016